T0284397

The Self: A Very Short Introduction

VERY SHORT INTRODUCTIONS are for anyone wanting a stimulating and accessible way into a new subject. They are written by experts, and have been translated into more than 45 different languages.

The series began in 1995, and now covers a wide variety of topics in every discipline. The VSI library currently contains over 750 volumes—a Very Short Introduction to everything from Psychology and Philosophy of Science to American History and Relativity—and continues to grow in every subject area.

Very Short Introductions available now:

ABOLITIONISM Richard S. Newman
THE ABRAHAMIC RELIGIONS
  Charles L. Cohen
ACCOUNTING Christopher Nobes
ADDICTION Keith Humphreys
ADOLESCENCE Peter K. Smith
THEODOR W. ADORNO
  Andrew Bowie
ADVERTISING Winston Fletcher
AERIAL WARFARE Frank Ledwidge
AESTHETICS Bence Nanay
AFRICAN AMERICAN HISTORY
  Jonathan Scott Holloway
AFRICAN AMERICAN RELIGION
  Eddie S. Glaude Jr
AFRICAN HISTORY John Parker and
  Richard Rathbone
AFRICAN POLITICS Ian Taylor
AFRICAN RELIGIONS
  Jacob K. Olupona
AGEING Nancy A. Pachana
AGNOSTICISM Robin Le Poidevin
AGRICULTURE Paul Brassley and
  Richard Soffe
ALEXANDER THE GREAT
  Hugh Bowden
ALGEBRA Peter M. Higgins
AMERICAN BUSINESS HISTORY
  Walter A. Friedman
AMERICAN CULTURAL HISTORY
  Eric Avila
AMERICAN FOREIGN RELATIONS
  Andrew Preston
AMERICAN HISTORY Paul S. Boyer

AMERICAN IMMIGRATION
  David A. Gerber
AMERICAN INTELLECTUAL
  HISTORY
  Jennifer Ratner-Rosenhagen
THE AMERICAN JUDICIAL SYSTEM
  Charles L. Zelden
AMERICAN LEGAL HISTORY
  G. Edward White
AMERICAN MILITARY HISTORY
  Joseph T. Glatthaar
AMERICAN NAVAL HISTORY
  Craig L. Symonds
AMERICAN POETRY David Caplan
AMERICAN POLITICAL HISTORY
  Donald Critchlow
AMERICAN POLITICAL PARTIES
  AND ELECTIONS L. Sandy Maisel
AMERICAN POLITICS
  Richard M. Valelly
THE AMERICAN PRESIDENCY
  Charles O. Jones
THE AMERICAN REVOLUTION
  Robert J. Allison
AMERICAN SLAVERY
  Heather Andrea Williams
THE AMERICAN SOUTH
  Charles Reagan Wilson
THE AMERICAN WEST
  Stephen Aron
AMERICAN WOMEN'S HISTORY
  Susan Ware
AMPHIBIANS T. S. Kemp
ANAESTHESIA Aidan O'Donnell

Available soon:

For more information visit our website

www.oup.com/vsi/

Marya Schechtman

THE SELF

A Very Short Introduction

OXFORD
UNIVERSITY PRESS

Great Clarendon Street, Oxford, OX2 6DP,
United Kingdom

Oxford University Press is a department of the University of Oxford.
It furthers the University's objective of excellence in research, scholarship,
and education by publishing worldwide. Oxford is a registered trade mark of
Oxford University Press in the UK and in certain other countries

Published in the United States of America by Oxford University Press
198 Madison Avenue, New York, NY 10016, United States of America

British Library Cataloguing in Publication Data
Data available

Library of Congress Control Number: 2023943528

ISBN 978-0-19-883525-7

Printed and bound by
CPI Group (UK) Ltd, Croydon, CR0 4YY

Contents

Preface

"Know thyself" is said to have been one of the maxims carved into the Temple of Apollo at Delphi. On the face of it, this does not seem like a very difficult task. My self is with me at every moment of every day, I have access to its inner thoughts and feelings, and I am hardly liable to mistake someone else for me. At the same time, the self is surprisingly elusive and opaque. What, after all, is a self? Is it some kind of object? If so, what kind? If not an object, what then? Is our sense of self ultimately illusory? Something that disappears when studied too closely? Our understanding of the self is replete with puzzles and paradoxes: I cannot be anyone but who I am, and yet everyone will acknowledge that there are circumstances in which being oneself is extremely difficult. If I change enough, I can be said to have become someone else, and yet I somehow remain to deal with the consequences of the alteration. I cannot get away from myself, and yet I can find and lose myself.

Some of these seeming mysteries can be addressed just by getting clearer on our terminology and making sure we use the word "self" consistently. Beneath most of these puzzles, however, are deep and pervasive questions about who and what we are and how we fit into the world. These are questions we address in one way or another throughout our lives, sometimes reflectively and sometimes just in the way we live. They have been core foci of major world religions and are a prevalent theme in literary and popular fiction, poetry, and pop songs. They have been explored in multiple fields of academic study, including philosophy, anthropology, psychology, sociology, and neuroscience, to name just a few, and they are discussed on talk shows, in coffeeshops, and during late night conversations with friends.

In what follows we will look at some of the most compelling and puzzling questions about the self, exploring them through an interdisciplinary lens. We will ask what kind of object a self is, if it is an object at all. We will consider what it means to be oneself, and why it is important, discuss what kinds of changes the self can and cannot survive, and puzzle about when a person can "become someone else." We will see what can be learned by looking at the development of the self, investigate the disordered self, through reflection on psychological and neurological conditions that involve spilt, incoherent, or disintegrating selves, and consider the role of the natural and social world in constituting and maintaining the self. As we consider the self from these different perspectives, we will find it to be something of a moving target. The "self" that is the focus of metaphysical investigation may or may not be the same "self" we are talking about when we say that someone is not being herself, which may be a different "self" yet from the one developmental psychologists investigate. There is no doubt that we operate with many conceptions of the self, and that conceptions of the self and its importance have varied both over time and across cultures. Considering some of the key debates about the "self" in different contexts will reveal, however, that there are important points of contact among these different conceptions, and investigating these will offer important insights. We may not find definitive answers to all (or any) of the questions we raise but exploring them seriously can allow us to make progress in following the oracle's mysterious injunction.

Acknowledgments

I have benefited greatly from the help of many friends and colleagues while writing this book. I am indebted to Daniel Cervone, Shaun Gallagher, Rami Gabriel, Dan McAdams, and Dan Zahavi for generously sharing their expertise. I am also deeply grateful to Marc Slors, Will Small, and Miriam Solomon for their sensitive and insightful feedback on earlier drafts, and to my family and my colleagues at UIC for their support and encouragement.

Chapter 1
The metaphysical self

Imagine waking up one morning, rubbing the sleep from your eyes, and finding a strange face looking back at you from your mirror. No matter what you do to try to wake yourself, and no matter how many different mirrors you try, the result is always the same. Such an experience might make you doubt your senses or your sanity, but it is unlikely to make you doubt that you are you. It is not even clear what it would mean to doubt that. While this scenario is far-fetched, it is by no means unfamiliar. Such "body swaps" make up the plot of countless stories, from folktales to science fiction, to Disney films like *Freaky Friday*. Millennia of religious and spiritual traditions have suggested that we can survive the death of our biological bodies, and people regularly report experiencing separation from their physical bodies in phenomena like astral projection and near-death experiences. As I write, there are researchers working on methods to upload the self to a computer so that we can continue without physical embodiment.

All of this suggests that at some fundamental level we take ourselves to be something other than, and potentially separable from, our bodies. We are not simply animals or organisms, but *selves*, which inhabit organisms or bodies but can come apart from them. This leaves us with the question of what kind of "something" a self is. This is a metaphysical question about the self. It asks what kind of entity a self is, how we can individuate selves (how would you count the number of selves in a room?), and how to tell when we are dealing with the same self at different times. These may seem like rather simple questions, but as we will see, they are not.

Soul survivor

The kinds of cases with which this chapter opened are often taken to suggest that a self is a seat of conscious experience which, although typically encountered attached to a human body, can be detached from it. One obvious and historically significant candidate for the kind of thing that might act as such a seat of consciousness is a soul. If this answer is to illuminate the nature of the self, however, we will need to know something more about what a soul is. Often when we talk about someone's soul—for instance when we say that "the eyes are the window to the soul" or that someone is a "gentle soul"—we use the word to talk about someone's nature or character. In the metaphysical context, however, it typically means something different. Here the soul is not the collection of traits and properties that define someone's nature, but rather the "something" that possesses those traits and properties. Just as physical traits require a physical substance or "substratum" that possesses them, so mental traits require a mental entity to possess them. If we encounter a red, ripe, round tomato, it is the *tomato* that is red and ripe and round. And when we encounter a self who thinks and feels and believes certain things, there should be a corresponding *substratum*, or basic "something," that possesses the thoughts, feelings, and beliefs. The idea of the soul usually invoked in this context is that of an immaterial substance that serves as such a substratum.

Those who hold that the self is a soul of this kind would see the case described at the beginning of this chapter as one in which a soul becomes separated from its original body and comes to inhabit a different one, carrying its subjectivity and psychological

2

attributes with it. While this does provide an answer to the question of what kind of thing a self is, there are several worries that have been raised about this approach. Many find the notion of an immaterial *thing* extremely mysterious if not downright incoherent. Objectors point out, moreover, that there is no need to have recourse to immaterial substance to account for the existence of the human mind. Developments in the scientific study of the mind, particularly neuroscience, suggest that we can account for our mentality in terms of activity of the nervous system. We know that brain activity is implicated in conscious experience, the argument goes, so positing an independent kind of substance in which this experience inheres is at best redundant.

Supporters of the existence of immaterial souls argue that scientific explanation alone cannot account for all aspects of our experience. Neuroscience may promise to provide a very complete and compelling account of the mechanisms underlying conscious experience, but it is the wrong kind of explanatory scheme to capture the subjective, qualitative aspects of consciousness. Science, it is claimed, will never be able to describe what it is like to look out at a meadow on a warm summer's day with a melancholy nostalgia for one's youth. A neuroscientific explanation of such an experience cannot even capture the vibrant green of the grass (there is nothing green in the brain) or the quality of light (it's dark in there) or the hum of the insects (nothing humming), let alone the nostalgic melancholy. Neuroscience may tell us what is happening physically when these subjective experiences occur, and that physical activity may turn out to be necessary for experience, but some additional component is needed to make sense of the subjective quality of consciousness. The question of whether and how there could be a purely physical account of subjectivity has been called the "hard problem" in the philosophy of mind by David Chalmers. It is a hard problem indeed, and questions about whether and how the mind can be accounted for in purely material terms persist.

Our discussion of the soul arose from the observation that it seems possible for the self to transfer from one body to another or even to exist disembodied. This led us to the postulate of the self as a detachable "something." To the extent that the existence of souls is in peril, so too is this way of understanding cases like the one that opened this chapter. Further investigation of our reactions to cases of "body change," however, suggests that it was perhaps a wrong turn to think about selves as souls in the first place. These difficult questions about the nature and existence of souls may thus be less relevant to understanding the self than they first appear.

All you need is consciousness

John Locke makes a compelling argument that cases like the ones we have been considering are not best explained by thinking of the self as a soul. This argument is found in his discussion of personal identity over time, which is also a discussion of the identity of the self, since he sees "person" and "self" as two names for the same entity: "Where-ever a Man finds, what he calls *himself*," Locke says, "there I think another may say is the same *Person*." Locke says that to understand the conditions of the identity of the self we must know what a self is, and he provides two important answers to this question. One is that a self is "a thinking intelligent being, that has reason and reflection, and can consider itself as itself, the same thinking thing in different times and places . . ." The other is that "person" (and so "self") is a "forensic term" which belongs "only to intelligent Agents capable of a Law and Happiness and Misery." As Locke uses the term "forensic" it does not apply only to questions raised in the context of legal proceedings, but to a broad range of practical considerations and judgments. To say that "person" is a forensic term means that a person is the kind of being that is the appropriate object of moral praise and blame, responsibility, and deservingness, and that it is the self that is the object of our love, devotion, loyalty, or suspicion. Once this is understood, Locke says, it becomes clear that sameness of self, or

4

person, consists in sameness of consciousness rather than of substance, either material (the body) or immaterial (the soul).

To show this, Locke uses a series of hypothetical cases like the one with which we opened. He asks us, for instance, to imagine the consciousness of a prince entering the body of a cobbler. It is obvious, he says, that the individual with the cobbler's body and prince's consciousness is responsible for what the prince did before the switch and not for what the cobbler did. This is plausible. If the prince was a horrible tyrant whose subjects were about to execute him, it seems right that he should not get off the hook just by switching bodies. If the prince was a beloved, wise, and benevolent leader whose consciousness was placed into the body of a cobbler by a jealous sorcerer, the person in the cobbler's body would deserve the adoration and praise due to the prince and it is to this person that the subjects should turn for guidance and leadership. If the prince knew that his consciousness was going to enter the body of the cobbler he would try to arrange for the person with his (current) consciousness and the cobbler's (current) body to have access to his money and power after the transfer. The relationship the queen and princess have with the prince would be most naturally continued with the person in the cobbler's (erstwhile) body rather than the one in the prince's. These are the kinds of judgments we are standardly invited to make in science fiction stories, and it seems natural to do so. For these "forensic" reasons, Locke concludes that the self goes where consciousness goes.

So far this is familiar territory. Locke takes things a step further, however, arguing that parallel considerations show that if continuity of soul and continuity of consciousness were to diverge, the self would go with the consciousness rather than the soul. Recall that the "soul" in this context is a bare substratum, the "something" that possesses thoughts, feelings, and beliefs. The soul itself is not the benevolent or evil intentions it might possess any more than the tomato is its redness or ripeness. The very same tomato that was green and unripe last week can be red and ripe today, and so can the soul that contained dark thoughts and evil intentions earlier be filled now with happy thoughts and compassionate intentions. Locke thus argues that there is no reason to think that consciousness or mind cannot move from one soul to another just as easily as from one body to another. As the soul is understood here, we can imagine someone waking up in a different immaterial soul from the one he went to sleep in in much the same way we imagined someone waking up in a different body than he went to sleep in. The main difference is that one can (in most instances) tell if one wakes up in a new body. Since souls are not detectable by the senses, there is no obvious way to know if one has changed souls. Perhaps we do it all the time.

It might be tempting to think of the self as the soul plus the consciousness it carries and require that both be transferred to a new body for the self to move. Locke's point, however, is that if we require sameness of consciousness, the soul does no real work in our definition. From this perspective, the role of the soul in the identity of the self is akin to the role of the storage medium in the identity of an electronic file. If I get a new computer and copy my files to it before wiping the old computer's memory completely, I still have all my files. They have been transferred to my new computer. Similarly, on Locke's account, if one's consciousness moves from one body or soul to another, one's self moves with it. We don't need the same soul for the same self any more than we need the original hard drive for the same files. This is directly connected to Locke's characterization of selves as forensic beings. Selves are the proper objects of our praise and blame, Locke argues, and it does not make sense to praise and blame someone for the *stuff* in which his dastardly intentions or saintly compassion occur. It is the intentions or compassion themselves that matter. Locke's view is in many ways quite radical. Before considering some of its broader implications, it will be helpful to look at developments of his basic approach in more recent discussions.

Technological complications

Starting in around the 1960s, there was renewed interest in Locke's account of personal identity, engendering a host of views inspired by his basic insights. Given the widespread acceptance of some form of materialism (the view that there is only material substance, and that immaterial substance does not exist) among those involved, the focus in these more recent discussions has been on showing that sameness of self does not require and is not entailed by sameness of body, with less attention given to the possibility that the self might be an immaterial soul. The kinds of imaginary cases offered to demonstrate the possibility that a self might separate from the body to which it is attached have also been updated and multiplied.

Instead of a prince entering the body of a cobbler, for instance, we are asked to imagine a teleporter that scans and disintegrates an intergalactic traveler, reconstructing the traveler molecule-for-molecule (out of new matter) on a distant planet. Using this imagined technology, the advertising says, someone can travel very quickly to planets whose distance would make old-fashioned spaceship travel impossible in a single lifetime (and suspended animation is so tedious!). It is an assumption of these cases that building a molecule-for-molecule replica of the original traveler's brain and body guarantees that the person who steps out of the transporter at the destination would have all the same memories, beliefs, values, desires, and psychological traits as the person who stepped in on Earth. In other words, these cases, like that of the prince and cobbler, are understood to transfer the consciousness of the original person to a new body, in this case a replica of the one it originally inhabited.

One notable difference between the science fiction cases in current use and Locke's hypothetical cases is that the former include an imagined mechanism for the transfer of consciousness (e.g., the teleporter) whereas Locke simply says there is a transfer with no explanation of how it occurs. In principle, this should not make a substantive difference. Either the transfer of consciousness amounts to the transfer of the self or it does not. The details provided in the more recent cases, however, help to reveal some complications for the Lockean view that are less evident in his vaguer description of the case. One of the most important is the possibility of replication once the connection between self and substance is given up. The argument that the person in the replicated body who steps out of the teleporter booth on a distant planet is the same self who stepped in on Earth is basically that that person would have the same psychological relation to the Earth traveler as we each have to our later selves in uncontroversial, ordinary cases of survival. As we said at the outset, when I wake up in the morning, I know who I am, and finding I am in a different body from the one I went to sleep in does not shake that conviction. Similarly, the intergalactic traveler will awaken on a distant planet remembering himself getting into the teleporter, ready to make the presentation he came to make and then to pick up some souvenirs for the family and head home.

The problem is that once we imagine having this technology there is no obvious reason it could not be used to create multiple replicas of the original traveler on multiple planets, each connected to the person on Earth in the same way. Each, that is, would leave the teleporter booth on a different planet remembering the original person's life on Earth, taking the Earth person's family as her own, and intending to bring souvenirs back to the Earth person's children. It is deeply challenging for a view that defines continuity of the self in terms of sameness of consciousness (or, as it is more commonly called in the current discussion, "psychological continuity") to say what happens to the self in such a case. There are three logical possibilities, none of which is totally satisfying.

One is that the original self continues in *all* the people who exit the teleporter booths on other planets. It is difficult to make sense of this. Each of these teleporter products could live out their life on a different planet, never knowing of the others' existence. Or they could all show up at the same home or office after business is concluded, each claiming the same job or family and insisting, sincerely, that the others are imposters. There is no shared subjective experience among the travelers; none is directly aware of what the others are thinking and feeling. While we can perhaps make some sense of the idea of selves with divided consciousness (as we will discuss in Chapter 5), it seems to stretch the notion of self too far to say that all these beings with distinct consciousness, living different lives, could be a single self. If they are not the same self as one another, however, they cannot all be the same self as the original traveler who entered the booth on Earth. I cannot be the same self as a dozen distinct selves.

If the original traveler can be the same self as at most one of the people who step out of teleporter booths, perhaps she is the same as exactly one of the replicas. This makes formal sense, but it is difficult to defend this position. All the interplanetary travelers have precisely the same psychological relation to the person who entered on Earth. If it is sameness of consciousness that makes sameness of self as we have been supposing, there seems no justification whatsoever to choose one of these travelers over any other as the original traveler.

The final possibility is to say that none of the resulting selves is the same self as the original traveler. This possibility is suggested by the failures of the first two. If the self cannot be divided in the way the first interpretation requires, and it is not tenable to say that just one of the resulting people is the same as the original self, it must be that this kind of multiplication ends the original self and produces copies in its place. Just as we might say that an individual cell ceases to exist when it divides, giving rise to "daughter" cells that succeed it, we might say that someone multiplied in teleportation ceases to exist and is survived by a group of successor selves. While this is a strange result, it is in many ways the most metaphysically sound possibility. It is important to note, however, that ceasing to exist in this way is not the same thing as death. Cell division is not cell death, and the same could be said of self division.

Derek Parfit, who was instrumental in developing many of the puzzling cases concerning identity at the core of this discussion, makes this point explicitly. If we allow that making multiple copies of a self results in the original self ceasing to exist, he says, we must allow that this kind of cessation, unlike ordinary death, contains everything that matters to us in survival. His argument is straightforward. Teleportation without copies is just a version of the case of the prince and the cobbler and in this case, as in Locke's, we judge that the transfer of the traveler's consciousness to a different body on a distant planet carries the self to that planet and preserves what we care about in survival. It is hard to see how the existence of other copies of the self on other planets could undo that. The person who steps out of the teleportation booth on Mars has the same relation to the person on Earth whether there is also a replica on Venus or not. The existence of other copies of the self might complicate matters (perhaps they would compete for the same job or partner), or it might be beneficial (allowing for useful division of labor), but it does not seem like the kind of thing that could make the difference between surviving and not surviving.

Parfit's argument has been extremely influential. There are a variety of ways to resist his conclusion but one that is especially important is to turn Parfit's argument around on him. Parfit says that the fact that we have everything that matters in survival when there is a single copy of the original traveler implies that what matters must be present in each copy when more than one is produced. We might argue instead that what matters to survival is clearly *not* present in the case with multiple copies and since, as Parfit says, the relation to the original person is the same in the case where there is only one copy, we need to reconsider the assumption that the self survives even in the single-copy case. Interestingly, while people do seem overwhelmingly to judge that there is a transfer of self from one body to the other in the case of the prince and cobbler, or on Freaky Friday, reactions tend to be more mixed in the case of teleportation. This is likely because the specification of mechanism in the latter case makes explicit that the "transfer" is in fact an act of copying. Without sameness of substance, there is a sense in which this is really all it can be.

Once this aspect of the view is foregrounded, it is less convincing that having someone in the future related to one's current consciousness in this way is really a form of survival. There seems to be a deep and important difference between actually surviving and being disintegrated and replaced by a replica, just as there seems to be a real difference between surviving and being killed and replaced by someone with delusions that they are you, no matter how carefully they have studied your psychological life and no matter how closely they replicate it. But then what about the powerful reactions to the kind of hypothetical case that opened this chapter? What underlies our ambivalence, I think, is an ambiguity in the idea of "sameness of consciousness," one that is easier to recognize in the science fiction cases than in cases like Locke's. On the one hand, "consciousness" may be understood to name the mere fact of subjective awareness; on the other, it can be understood to mean the contents of our awareness, the specific beliefs, desires, memories, thoughts, perceptions, and so on that are part of consciousness and make up conscious experience. "Sameness of consciousness" means something different depending upon which understanding of "consciousness" is employed.

The difference is difficult to articulate, but important. One way of understanding it is to note that people can have similar *contents* of consciousness without having the *same* consciousness. If you and I have the same thought or I ask whether you saw what I saw, and we determine that you did, this does not mean that you and I are a single consciousness. I have no more access to your subjective experience than I would if you were having radically different experiences from mine. The sense in which you and I have the "same consciousness" or "same conscious states" is like the sense of sameness that is at work when I tell you, for example, that I have the same shirt you are wearing at home. I obviously do not have the very one you are wearing; mine is in a different location. What I mean is that I have one that is just like it. Philosophers call this "qualitative identity." This is contrasted with "numerical identity," which is in play when I recognize the shirt you are wearing as the very one I lent you last month, which you never returned. The worry in teleportation is that what is created in the replica is a numerically distinct consciousness that is qualitatively the same as the original, and that that is not the right kind of sameness to yield survival.

What I want when I hope to survive into the future, objectors say, is not for there to be someone in the future who has the exact same contents of consciousness as those I have now. Instead, I am hoping that *I* the conscious subject who is experiencing this desire to survive and fear I might not, will continue to have experiences in the future. I want my stream of consciousness to flow on, and it is not clear that teleportation provides this form of continuity. The fact that a teleported replica has qualitatively the same psychological make-up, walking out of the booth on a distant planet as I had walking in on Earth, does not guarantee that my stream of consciousness flows on in that person. This is what the case with multiple replicas helps us to see. It is extremely difficult to imagine what it would be for my current stream of consciousness to flow on in multiple teleportation products spread across the galaxy. There is no unified first-person point of view in this scenario in which the experiences had by all these replicas occur. If we have reason to think that the original person's consciousness would not flow on in multiple replicas, however, we also have reason to think that it would not flow on when there is only one, since the relation to that one replica remains the same whether there are others or not. The worry is thus that in teleportation my stream of consciousness abruptly ends when I am disintegrated on Earth and one or more replicas with delusions of having my history are created. It is not a means of travel; it is death.

Are there selves?

Because we do not have replicators, in our actual experience the level of moment-to-moment similarity in contents of consciousness that is present between the prince before the switch and the cobbler after, or between the traveler and her replica, occurs only within the life of a single individual (and even then, this kind of exact similarity would occur only in closely proximate moments), and so only within a single stream of consciousness. The initial judgment that a person switches bodies in cases like the prince and the cobbler or teleportation without replicas may thus rest on an implicit assumption that where this kind of sameness in the contents of consciousness is present, so too is continuation of the same experiencing subject. Once we recognize this, we may feel that it is only in cases where consciousness actually flows on that the original person survives. Locke's original insight can thus be preserved by making it explicit that sameness of self is constituted by the continued flow of the same conscious subject of experience or first-person point of view rather than by the sameness of the contents of consciousness (i.e., the particular beliefs, values, desires, intentions, and psychological traits). There are some problems with this approach, however.

To begin, this revised account no longer captures some of the most compelling parts of Locke's original argument. Recall that the basis of his argument that the continuity of substance, even an immaterial soul, is neither sufficient nor necessary for sameness of person is that mere continuity of stuff, without the continuation of memories, beliefs, intentions, and so on, cannot provide the basis for praise and blame and other practical ("forensic") judgments associated with sameness of the self. If we sharply distinguish between sameness of experiencing subject at two different times and qualitative similarity in the contents of consciousness at those times, it is not obvious why sameness of experiencing subject without similarity in the contents of consciousness should be any more relevant to judgments of praise and blame than sameness of soul is. That the stream of consciousness of the prince flows on in the cobbler's body but with none of the prince's wisdom or memories or benevolence does not seem enough to make the person in the cobbler's body worthy of praise for what the prince did, nor is this person especially well prepared to rule the kingdom or engage with the queen and princess.

Moreover, if we reject the idea that continuation of the self involves a continuing substance, it is not at all obvious what it could mean for sameness of consciousness or first-person point of view to flow on above and beyond the fact that we retain many of our memories, beliefs, desires, and traits. Cases of replication evoked a strong sense that we are after more in survival than just having someone in the future who is psychologically like us. That someone will have experiences like mine in the future is not a consolation. *I* want to have experiences. Parfit challenges us, however, to describe a difference between these two outcomes that could make a difference of the sort we are after. He argues that if the presence or absence of a single experiencing subject or stream of consciousness is what distinguishes between surviving and ceasing to exist, it will have to be a difference that is experienced by someone. On the picture we are trying to capture, it must be *experientially* different for me to continue than it is for me to be replaced by a replica. Although he does not put it in quite these terms, the fundamental challenge Parfit poses is to make sense of such an experiential difference and to say who experiences it.

In the teleportation case, for instance, the difference between surviving teleportation and only appearing to survive is not something that would be experienced by the person stepping into the booth on Earth, since nothing has happened yet. But it won't be experienced by the replica either. By hypothesis, the person exiting on (say) Mars will think that she is the person who left Earth just a few minutes ago and be happy to have made it to Mars to get on with her work there. Who, then, would experience the difference between survival and replication? And if no one experiences it, how can it be an experiential difference? We might protest that this way of putting the challenge involves a trick. The reason we cannot point to who is experiencing the difference is precisely because the person who might have has ceased to exist. If death is oblivion, then we do not experience ordinary death (as it occurs in the real world) either, but that does not mean there is no experiential difference between surviving and dying. If there is an afterlife in which consciousness flows on after our bodies die, then the Earth traveler who is disintegrated in the teleporter can be imagined experiencing our universe from afar, disembodied and following the adventures of the replica who has taken her place.

While this does seem to get at what is frustrating in Parfit's challenge, he can rightly press the matter here by asking why we are so sure that the disembodied continuer in the case just described is the same experiencing subject as the original, or that the stream of consciousness flows on in her rather than in the embodied replica on Mars. She *thinks* she is the original person, but so does the replica. Neither has the same body or brain as the original person. Perhaps we are assuming that her disembodied existence implies that her soul has continued, but we have already argued that this will not settle the matter of where the self is either. If continued flow of the same subject of experience is to be defined in experiential terms rather than in terms of continuity of substance or of the contents of consciousness, we need to be able to say something about what that experiential difference is, and it seems to evaporate when we look for it. After analyzing the situation, Parfit reaches the radical conclusion that there is no deep difference between survival and replacement because the experiential connection we have to our future selves is precisely the same as that we would have to a replica. Ordinary survival, he concludes, is as good as being replaced by a replica, not because our connection to a replica would be as deep as the connection we take ourselves to have to our future selves in ordinary survival, but because the connection we actually have to our future selves is as superficial as that we would have to a replica. We think there is a deep fact about survival of the experiencing self with important implications, but this is not the case. All we have is qualitative similarity.

There are some ways to resist Parfit's radical conclusion. One is to insist that the fact that we cannot articulate the difference between genuine continuity and replacement with a replica does not mean that no such difference exists. It may be a brute fact that cannot be explained or described in more basic terms, just as there is not much to say in response to the question of what makes "1 = 1" true. This view has been offered and defended frequently, but many find it unsatisfying since it makes the self a mystery and leaves us with no way ever to really know who we are.

Another possibility is to reject the legitimacy of the method of hypothetical cases for exploring these questions. One oft-cited worry is that our reactions to these stories can be easily manipulated by the way the story is told, making them inconsistent and untrustworthy. We might also ask why our reactions to these cases should be taken to tell us what is truly involved in the continuation of selves rather than merely showing what we think is involved. The fact that, until recently, there was very little systematic collection of cross-cultural reactions to these cases adds to these worries and raises the question of whether they can say anything truly general about the self. Many philosophers have also argued that reflection on cases involving transformations that are impossible in the real world cannot tell us much about the nature and continuity of selves like ours. A world with teleportation or body swaps or replication would contain very different beings than ours, and what is true about the identity of those kinds of selves may not be true about the identity of our selves. This methodological argument, if successful, shows that we need not accept conclusions that are supported directly and exclusively by such cases, but it does not tell us much about what a self is, or what is required for one to continue.

Parfit acknowledges that many will find his conclusions difficult to accept but is quick to point out that the idea that there is no self of the sort we generally believe there to be is hardly a new idea. In philosophy, for instance, it can be found in the work of David Hume, among others. It is also, Parfit notes, part of many Asian traditions, including Buddhism, as well as Western popularizations of those traditions, and various forms of mysticism. The claim that selves are illusory has a long and storied history.

We need to attend carefully, however, to what is actually being denied in denying the reality of the self, which is not necessarily the same for all such denials. In some cases, the claim seems to amount to the rejection of a separately existing substance like a soul, or a particular brain region, which underwrites the unity of consciousness. This does not rule out the existence of selves understood as experiential unities of consciousness, and so is not immediately relevant to this debate. Some in the "no self" tradition do reject the idea of a persisting experiential unity, and so offer a more direct challenge to traditional accounts of the self as unified subjects of experience. Given that most people report a strong experience of themselves as ongoing unified subjects, those who deny the existence of this form of experience need to argue somehow that we are not experiencing what we think we are. This is a difficult argument to make. One form it can take is the one we see in Parfit in which, after arguments are offered to make the notion of such a self problematic, we are directed to introspect and really attend to our experience. If we do, it is argued, we will find it less fixed than we thought. There have also been some interesting recent attempts to loosen the hold of our conviction that we truly experience ourselves as unified through findings in neuroscience. This approach points to details about the way in which sensory input from both our bodies and the external world is processed in the brain, arguing that the input we get is rapidly fluctuating and that there is no locus in our brains where everything that is in our consciousness is integrated into a flow of stable, ongoing experience.

What is probably the most common form of argument against the idea of the self as a unified subject does not deny that we *do* experience ourselves as unified, ongoing selves, only that we must *inevitably* do so. This approach argues that the experience of unity is generated by attitudes that can be overcome through methods like mediation, reflection, or the use of psychoactive chemicals. This is usually connected to the corollary that overcoming this illusion is beneficial, freeing us from anxieties, suffering, and isolation. This point is emphasized by Parfit. He acknowledges that some may find it depressing to discover that their connection to a future self is no deeper than their connection to a replica would be, but says that he finds it liberating, diminishing fears of future pain and death, and making him feel less cut off from others. This idea is part of many traditions that urge practices aimed at freeing oneself from the experience of a continuing self.

Even if we accept all of this, it does not necessarily imply that the unity of the experiencing subject, when it does occur, is illusory. The need to undertake intensive practices to free ourselves from this form of experience shows, on the contrary, that it is very robust. This approach thus does not really show that selves understood as experiencing subjects are not real. It does, however, argue that their existence is not necessary and depends at least to some degree upon our attitudes. This is a significant claim. If the unity of conscious subject is something contingent, we have reason to try to understand the conditions under which it arises and how it is maintained. If, as tradition has it, these subjects are selves, this amounts to understanding how selves come to be.

While our metaphysical questions about the nature of the self and the conditions of its continuity have offered few definitive conclusions, they have provided insight and raised valuable questions. We have seen both the appeal and the challenges of the view of the self as a unified subject of experiences. We have also seen a distinction between a single conscious subject of experience flowing on (let's call this "basic continuity of consciousness") and the qualitative similarity of contents of consciousness over time, and registered difficulties with getting a handle on the former. Finally, we noted the suggestion that basic continuity of consciousness is something that must be actively generated and maintained through our attitudes.

Chapter 2
Becoming someone else

It is not uncommon in everyday life to remark that someone has become "a different person" or turned into "someone else." Such claims do not, however, appear to mean quite the same thing in everyday speech as they do in the cases discussed in the previous chapter. Investigating what they do mean and how they might be connected to the questions raised in Chapter 1 will illuminate an important strain of thought about the self, raise fruitful questions for further exploration, and provide additional insight into some of the questions that arose in that discussion.

Everyday transformations

There is a wide range of real-life circumstances in which we might say that someone has become a different self. Someone might exclaim with satisfaction that she is a whole new person after a shower and a hot cup of coffee. Parents might say (with pride, dismay, or a mixture of both) that their child has come back from university as someone else (or the child might insist that he has become a new person at university despite his parents' refusal to recognize it). We might say that someone has become a different person since winning the lottery or after a divorce or as the result of a religious conversion, trauma, or medical intervention. Everyday language is not always precise, and the variety of circumstances in this brief list shows that the cases in which we talk about a change of self can differ from one another along many dimensions. It is therefore not to be expected that reflection on everyday cases of becoming a new self will reveal a clear and consistent set of criteria for when this happens. We can, however, still learn a great deal by thinking about these cases.

None of these cases is quite like those we considered in the metaphysical discussion. Rather than prince-and-cobbler-style scenarios in which an entire, unchanged psychological life is imagined moving from one body to another, they focus on qualitative change in personality, beliefs, values, desires, and plans within a single human life. These ordinary claims of a change in self do not, for the most part, seem to suggest that someone has become a different person in the literal, metaphysical sense at issue in the previous chapter. In fact, their force seems to depend on the presupposition of a single, continuing self within whom change takes place. It matters that my beloved uncle has become a "different person" after his accident because he is in some sense still my uncle and his change is disturbing. It is gratifying to see that my friend has become a new person since she got out of that terrible relationship because there is some basic sense in which she is my friend throughout. I care about her, and so I am pleased by how her life has improved and happy that she is so much more confident, joyful, and assertive now.

While all of this is true, it is worth considering why we are tempted to use metaphors of "identity" or "becoming a new self" in describing these everyday changes, and whether the fact that we do signifies an important connection between a more literal sense of "self" and the one at work in everyday contexts. The sense of "metaphorical" here will necessarily be left somewhat vague. To get us started, however, we can say that if a case in which we say someone has become a different person presupposes a more fundamental kind of persistence in the ways described above, it can be provisionally seen as metaphorical. Everyday cases of "becoming someone else" can be put on a rough continuum from

21

those that are clearly metaphorical (those that obviously presuppose a more basic unity) to those that suggest a change of self in a more fundamental sense, one that in the end is perhaps not so cleanly distinguishable from the one at work in the metaphysical discussion.

Someone who says she has been made a new person by a shower and coffee is speaking hyperbolically and probably means no more than that she feels a lot better. Saying that someone has become a different person at university, or since winning the lottery or getting a divorce, seems to indicate something more. The change noted is deeper and more lasting, but still seems clearly to presuppose a more basic continuity. In some of the more extreme cases in which we talk about lost identity, a veteran who returns from battle with Post-Traumatic Stress Disorder (PTSD), someone who exhibits marked changes after a stroke or personality-changing medical intervention, or someone who undergoes a major religious conversion, it is no longer clear that the claims are entirely metaphorical, although they also do not seem quite literal. Closer examination of these cases will thus help us understand the ways in which the continuity of self at issue in these claims is distinct from and related to the more fundamental, literal form of continuity discussed in the previous chapter.

You've changed

It will be useful to have in hand a fairly detailed description of some cases of real-life change at the more literal end of the spectrum. Here are three representative examples:

The first is profound personality change resulting from a traumatic experience. By now the phenomenon of PTSD is widely known, and there is a fair bit of familiarity with some of its main symptoms, including flashbacks, anxiety, nightmares, intrusive thoughts, and difficulty readjusting to day-to-day life. Trauma that results in PTSD is something that tends to break life into a "before" and "after." There are, sadly, a great many examples of this condition. A clear and poignant expression of how it can be seen to make someone a different person is found in a National Post interview with the father of a Canadian soldier who suffered PTSD after serving in Afghanistan and ultimately committed suicide. The piece describes Jamie, a fun-loving, happy young man, the life of the party, with "a huge heart and the lasting friendships to prove it," who went off to be a soldier and returned shattered, "engulfed by despair" and prone to unpredictable angry outbursts. His father says that he returned home "practically unrecognizable," that "Jamie never came home. A different person came back from Afghanistan."

A quite different kind of transformation, although one that brings about similar judgments, can be found in some cases of Deep Brain Stimulation (DBS). Originally a treatment for Parkinson's, DBS involves the placement of electrodes in the brain. A box outside of the body provides a switch which, when flipped, results in electrical stimulation to the parts of the brain in which the electrodes are placed. In treating Parkinson's patients, it was discovered that this modality sometimes had effects on mood and personality, and that it could also be effective for a variety of psychiatric disorders, including previously treatment-resistant depression and obsessive-compulsive disorder. Sometimes (by no means always) the results are truly astounding. There are cases in which patients with long-term, disabling depression are utterly transformed the moment the switch is flipped. In these cases, patients who had been incapacitated by depression for decades, barely able to function, in an instant became joyful and energetic.

One case involved a profoundly depressed patient suddenly "laughing and talking about eating croissants and going to an aerobics class." Another patient describes how with the flip of a switch everything in the room became brighter, and his depression simply vanished. As welcome as these changes are, they are also disconcerting for those who undergo and witness them. Patients, their loved ones, and even medical personnel have described the changes as frightening and disorienting. Frequently the profound change brought about by DBS when it works in this way engenders friction with family, friends, and employers, who explain that they must suddenly deal with a "whole new person" from the one with whom they were interacting before the procedure. In a study of the personality effects of DBS one patient (who was treated for Parkinson's Disease and not depression) says that she did not feel like the *me* who went into surgery, and that her family grieves for old "me."

A final example is found in conversion experiences. There are a great many well-known examples of conversion. Saul of Tarsus, a persecutor of the early Christians, is struck on the road to Damascus and becomes the Apostle Paul. Siddhartha leaves the palace, witnesses suffering, and becomes the Buddha. Malcolm X undergoes a jailhouse conversion and joins the Nation of Islam. Each of these conversions, and many others like them, involve vast changes in goals, conduct, beliefs, intentions, and desires. The profound nature of these changes is signaled by the fact that they are often called "rebirths," and it is significant that each of the examples just given involves taking a new name. Frequently old relationships are severed, and old habits and activities are exchanged for new ones.

It is important to acknowledge that not only are there significant differences among these three kinds of cases, but also a great deal of variation within each kind. Not everyone who is traumatized develops PTSD, and this condition has varying degrees of severity and outcome. Relatively few cases of DBS involve the kind of instantaneous and profound changes I described, and there are gradations and differences in the personality effects of this treatment. Conversions can be immediate or gradual and involve more or less profound change. Nevertheless, dramatic change does occur in some of these cases, and when it does, it is common for both those who undergo the change and those who interact with them to describe this in terms of their becoming someone else. In these contexts, it is not obvious that the claim is entirely metaphorical. Identifying the features of these extreme cases which make them seem to veer towards a literal change of self (and determining in what sense, if any, they fall short of literal change) will thus reveal a great deal about the idea of self at work here and its relation to that discussed in the previous chapter.

Two features

One way of thinking about the continuum from an "identity-changing" shower to more serious cases of transformation is in terms of the quantity and duration of change. The more someone changes, the more literally we are likely to take the claim that they have become someone else. This does not tell us much, however, without more information about the metric to be used for measuring the amount of change. What exactly does it mean to say that someone has changed "a lot"? One straightforward possibility is suggested by Parfit, who addresses this question within the metaphysical debate about persons. He emphasizes that psychological change can be a matter of degree, and that the degree of change affects our judgments of personal identity. If someone changes in just one or two beliefs, desires, values, intentions, or traits, he says, we are unlikely to think that this has any effect on identity. If they change in 95 percent of these states, we are likely to think they have become literally someone else (at least according to Parfit, remember that he does not believe there is such a thing as basic continuity of consciousness). On this view, it is just a matter of counting the brute number of psychological features lost or retained.

This straightforward approach has its advantages but does not seem very promising once we ask how we are to individuate and count these kinds of psychological features. Take a teenager in love with a pop idol who reads something in a magazine that makes her love him a bit less. Is this a change in psychological state or not? Suppose she comes to love a different idol instead. Is this one psychological change (the object of her affection) or two (falling out of love with idol one and falling in love with idol two) or none (she is still prone to crushes of this sort)? Suppose she later stops falling in love with idols altogether and starts thinking about a relationship with a person in her social orbit. How many changes is that? Suppose after some time she realizes that she is not heterosexual and takes on a new gender identity, one at odds with her deep religious convictions. Is that the same number of changes as changing her affections from one idol to another? As changing from idols to more realistic objects of affection? And if the absolute number of states changed is the same in each case, does that really mean that these changes count the same towards our (or her) assessment of whether she is the same self?

It is just not clear what makes a single psychological feature, and not all psychological features appear to play the same role in determining the identity of the self. For these reasons, a simple ledger of changes is difficult to produce and, even if produced, would be unlikely to capture the variations in magnitude of change that we are looking for. The observations just made and the cases we have considered can, together, help us articulate at least two features of the nature of psychological change which seem important in determining the extent to which it brings about a new self.

The first is that some parts of our psychological make-up are more central to our identities than others. This is hardly a revelation and most of us probably take it for granted that this is the case. It suggests, however, a notion of "self" distinct from the metaphysical or literal one that plays an important role in our thought about what a self is. This is the familiar idea of a "true" or "deep" self (I will use these terms interchangeably). The basic thought is that, while we all have a great many traits, habits, beliefs, desires, preferences, intentions, plans, and goals, some of these are rather peripheral, while others go to the very core of our identity. If these core features change, we become in some sense unrecognizable to ourselves and others, as Jamie did when he came back from Afghanistan, and as radically altered DBS patients and converts often do.

We might thus think that there is a unified set of psychological features that define a true self and must be maintained for that self to continue. The next chapter will examine this notion of the true self more thoroughly, raising complications and suggesting refinements. For present purposes, however, the general idea of a distinction between core and peripheral traits is all we need. This allows us to arrange cases of real-life psychological change along the spectrum from metaphorical to literal changes in identity depending upon whether their effects are on peripheral or core traits. The kinds of changes a shower and cup of coffee can bring about are unlikely to be changes in the true self. Changes engendered by a divorce or life-changing windfall might or might not be. People do sometimes say that that they "don't know who they are" in such circumstances (think, for instance, of Nora at the end of Ibsen's *A Doll's House*), but in many cases they integrate the new circumstances into their current lives and carry on. PTSD, DBS, and conversion, at least the instances we have been discussing, seem very likely to involve significant changes in the true self. The core features that defined the earlier selves in these cases are so thoroughly altered that they may be thought no longer to be the same true self, something with profound consequences for them and for those who interact with them.

A second feature that inclines us to judge these changes as generating something like a literal change of self is their profound impact on an individual's activities and relationships. Real-life cases towards the literal end of the spectrum involve severe disruption of a human life. Those who suffer from PTSD are frequently unable to reconnect with old friends and their relationships with their families change. They have difficulty returning to their old jobs or holding new ones; they no longer take joy in old hobbies and pastimes. Changes are more positive in the relevant cases of DBS, but can be just as disruptive. Those who undergo radical psychological alteration with alleviation of symptoms often have similar difficulties negotiating relationships with family and friends and frequently have problems at work as well. There is also a whole new set of activities and relationships available after the intervention (recall the woman who is suddenly interested in aerobics and croissants). Conversion, we noted, is often explicitly described as starting a new life, severing past ties and establishing new ones, giving up old ways and taking a new path. In each of these cases there is a "before" and "after," a turning point after which the thread of the life lived before is not picked up again. This feature also seems to be at work more generally, but to a lesser extent, along the early points of the spectrum of "becoming someone else." The woman who has had her shower and coffee is now able to interact with people and undertake activities in a way she could not in her unwashed, uncaffeinated state. A divorce or windfall will disrupt many aspects of life that will need to be repaired or reimagined moving forward. The disruption in these cases is less than in the extreme cases, however, which is what places them earlier in the spectrum.

Life-altering change

I said earlier that although real-life judgments that someone has become a different self do not seem to involve claims of a literal change of identity, in the extreme cases these judgments do not seem entirely metaphorical either. We are now in a better position to consider in what sense this might be so. To begin, we can see why claims of a new identity appear to be metaphorical even in extreme real-life cases by noting that these cases seem to presuppose a more basic continuity, and so to meet the provisional criterion given at the beginning of the chapter. Part of the cruelty of Jamie's suffering when he returns from Afghanistan is that he recognizes his family and friends as his and remembers his happy-go-lucky life. The problem is that he cannot recapture or relate to any of it. DBS patients recognize their transformations as the result of a treatment they were seeking for a long-standing illness, understanding that *they* once suffered from symptoms that have vastly improved. Similarly, converts are only *converts* if they are at some level the same person who was lost in sin. Otherwise, their conversion would not count as "redemption" or "spiritual growth." In this way, some more literal form of continuation seems to be in place despite the radical change.

In what sense, then, might the changes in the extreme real-life cases be seen as literal (or "almost" literal)? A good strategy for answering this question is to return to the two features we identified as distinguishing extreme cases from more ordinary ones—the change in core features of the true self and the disruption of the thread of a life—to see if they can illuminate why these cases seem "not entirely metaphorical." The first of these does not help very much with this task. The fact that changes affect the true self may make them especially profound and poignant, but it is not obvious that this makes them any more literal. This fact does not, for instance, make these kinds of changes obviously like those observed in the case of the prince and cobbler, which was offered as a paradigmatic example of a literal change of self in Chapter 1. The cobbler's body with the prince's consciousness does not take itself to have any history with the cobbler's family (as the self in Jamie's body takes himself to have with his) and remembers nothing whatsoever of the cobbler's previous life (as, e.g., the DBS patient remembers signing up for treatment or the convert remembers his sinful life). So, a kind of continuity of self remains present in even the most extreme real-life cases of becoming someone else that does not seem to be present in cases widely recognized as involving a literal change in self.

The relevant difference between the real-life cases and cases like the prince and cobbler seems to rest on something like the distinction between basic continuity of consciousness and qualitative continuity of the contents of consciousness discussed in the previous chapter. To the extent that we accept that there is such a thing as basic continuity of consciousness, as many do, there is no clear reason to assume that it is absent in any of the extreme real-life cases. The kinds of connections that remain and the basic comportment of the individuals involved suggest that the same experiencing subject is present before and after the change in these cases in a way that does not seem to be the case in the "body-switch" scenarios. Focusing on the fact that these cases involve a change in the true self thus seems to reinforce the idea that the sense in which one becomes someone else through such changes is, after all, metaphorical. From this perspective, these cases seem like an especially important kind of psychological change that takes place within the life of a single experiencing subject, yielding qualitative change that does not amount to a literal change of self.

The second feature we identified as characteristic of the extreme cases, however, that they involve a severe disruption of the activities and relationships that make up a life, suggests an importantly different way of thinking about the literal identity of the self, and so sheds more light on the sense in which these cases seem to involve a literal change. So far, we have been operating implicitly with the widely held idea of the self as a fully psychological entity introduced in Chapter 1. A corollary of this idea is that the literal identity of the self will be determined by psychological factors. Our reflection on real-life extreme cases of change in self has, however, revealed another, extra-psychological, dimension of change that also seems to play an important role in establishing identity. In these cases, there is a stark before and after, an inability to connect with parts of one's past life in the ordinary way. Once this is recognized in the real-life context, we can see that it is present also in the case of the prince and cobbler, and that it also plays an important role in our judgments of a metaphysical change of self in that case.

If we recall the considerations elicited to show that the person with the cobbler's body and prince's consciousness is the same person as the prince, we will see that many of them revolve around which activities and relationships are natural to that person. We are directed to note that the person with the prince's consciousness in the cobbler's body is most naturally held accountable for actions of the prince, and not the cobbler, that he will naturally pick up relationships with the queen and princess, but not with the cobbler's wife and children, that he will be able to rule as the prince did, but not to make shoes. Similar considerations are offered in the original case of teleportation (with only one traveler) as reasons for thinking that the person who steps out of the booth on a distant planet is the one who stepped in on Earth. This person will carry out the business the traveler came to carry out and then return home to the traveler's friends and family, continuing the thread of her life. Although we later raised complications for the teleportation case, the initial reactions still reveal that the ability to seamlessly continue the activities and relationships of an earlier person is taken as important evidence that one is identical to that person, and that an inability to do so raises questions of identity.

The connection between real-life cases of psychological change at the extreme end of the spectrum and the case of the prince and cobbler with respect to the effects it has on a life lived points to a sense in which the former cases do not seem entirely metaphorical. Here, unlike with the change of true self, the changes we see in real life are of the same sort as the changes that are taken to undermine identity in the fantastic and science fiction cases used in metaphysical discussions. This does not necessarily imply that the real-life cases are literal changes in the self. Differences remain concerning the degree to which a life is disrupted in the fantastic cases and in the real ones. But this does seem like a genuine point of contact between literal and metaphorical changes in the identity of the self with many potential implications.

A defender of the view of the self as a purely psychological entity might argue that the ability to pick up the thread of a life is not itself essential to identity; it is merely evidence that the truly important feature, basic continuity of consciousness, is present. The inability to recognize the cobbler's wife and children or to make shoes shows us that the cobbler-body has lost its subjective connection to the consciousness of the cobbler, and with it the memories and knowledge necessary to shoemaking. The ability to interact with the princess and queen and to plan military campaigns, the argument might continue, shows that the person in that body has the consciousness that used to reside in the prince. The relation that actually makes the person in the cobbler body the one that used to be the prince is the continuity of consciousness, according to this argument, and not the ability to continue the thread of a life, which is merely a consequence of that, more basic, continuity.

It is not obvious, however, why we need to accept this analysis. Why not take the activities and relationships themselves to be part of what makes someone the same self? There are a variety of ways in which we might do this. One is to insist that it is actually the ability to pick up the thread of a life and *not* continuity of consciousness that determines metaphysical identity. Here the idea that continuity of activities and relationships constitute identity is offered as a competitor to the sameness of consciousness view offered in Chapter 1, one that aims to replace it. This is not a terrifically attractive option. Psychological and subjective features seem to be necessary elements of a self if anything is, and an account of the identity of the self that does not make any reference to such features seems highly implausible. A better option is to acknowledge the possibility that there may be more than one relation that is necessary for the identity of the self and to include the ability to continue the thread of a life as a part of what constitutes the literal identity of the self in addition to, rather than instead of, psychological and experiential factors.

An especially intriguing possibility involves thinking of these two forms of continuity not as distinct relations that together make up the continuity of the self, but rather as intertwined elements of a single, complex relation that defines identity. Continuity of consciousness and the ability to continue the thread of a life do seem to be interconnected. As defenders of the psychological approach point out, the ability to continue activities and relationships depends upon some level of continuity of consciousness. The conclusion they draw from this observation can be avoided, however, because the dependence plausibly goes the other direction as well. We have already noted that the idea of basic continuity of consciousness is elusive to the point where some question its very existence. At the end of Chapter 1, we also considered the possibility that this continuity of consciousness might need to be actively generated and maintained. If this is so, we might consider whether continuity in the activities and relationships that make up a life might play a role in bringing about and supporting this form of experience. This would make basic continuity of consciousness and the ability to pick up the thread of a life mutually interdependent. In other words, while disruptions of continuity of consciousness might undermine the ability to maintain activities and relationships, disruptions to activities and relationships might equally disrupt continuity of consciousness.

An advantage of this approach is that it gives us a strategy for getting clearer on what basic continuity of consciousness is and how it might be possible. We do not need to take it as a mysterious given fact but can understand it as a form of experience that is both built on and required for other kinds of continuities often associated with the self. We will see some reasons to endorse this idea and discover more details about how it might be developed in later chapters. First, however, it will be important to investigate the notion of the true self since it is clearly a significant piece of the overall puzzle.

Chapter 3
Being who you are

People are commonly advised to "just be themselves." Taken literally, there is not much need for this admonition; strictly speaking, there is no one else *you* could be. Yet people do find this advice useful, and sometimes surprisingly difficult to follow. This is because the "self" we are being urged to be is understood as the "true" or "deep" self introduced in the previous chapter, and because "being oneself" involves not just possessing traits, but also expressing them. We tend to think that who one presents, or even believes, oneself to be may not be who one really is deep down, that there is a genuine or authentic self that may or may not be expressed in what we do. Discovering and expressing the true self is taken to be deeply important, and many believe that being oneself in this sense is central to a fulfilled and happy life. Is there really such a thing as a true or deep self, though? If so, what kind of thing is it? What makes a trait or action expressive of who one "really is"?

Two truisms

One way to start thinking about what constitutes the true self is by considering two well-known truisms about circumstances in which people are not themselves. One is that people are often not themselves when they are inebriated or under extreme stress. If my friend snaps at me when she is under enormous pressure,

I may dismiss what she says, telling myself that she is just not herself with everything going on in her life. Similarly, if an acquaintance professes undying love during a night of heavy drinking, I may brush these declarations off on the grounds that it is not he, but the alcohol, speaking. The second truism is that you do not know who someone truly is until you see them in a disinhibited state or under pressure. A colleague who is typically polite might show her true colors, turning competitive and nasty when the layoffs start. Or perhaps the profession of undying love by a drunken friend is a classic case of *in vino veritas*. It is curious that both truisms really do ring true, since they seem to make exactly opposite claims. Each, moreover, expresses a widely held view of what constitutes the true self. In what follows we will consider what each of these views implies about the nature of the true self and whether there is any sense in which they can be made compatible. This will also involve questioning whether the idea that we each have a true self stands up to scrutiny.

My self, my choice

The main idea behind the claim that we are not ourselves when we are stressed or disinhibited is found in the bit of common wisdom Dumbledore shares with Harry Potter: "It is our choices, Harry, that show what we truly are, far more than our abilities." The suggestion is that the actions that express the true self are not involuntary behaviors or traits over which we have no control, but those undertaken deliberately. This has a great deal of plausibility. Suppose unexpected turbulence on an airplane causes me to stumble in the aisle, spilling coffee all over you. Or that I steal money from you after having been brainwashed by a cult leader who controls my every move. These cases, in different ways, involve events that, while occurring in my human history, do not result from my choices and so, on this view, do not reveal my true self. My fall during turbulence tells you more about the laws of physics than about me, and my illegal activities more about the true aims of the cult leader than about my true aims.

The truism that we are "not ourselves" when we are under stress or impaired suggests that these circumstances are relevantly like the more extreme cases just given, that what I do when stressed or inebriated also does not represent a genuine choice of mine. This claim requires some defense. There are real differences among the cases I have described, which means that seeing them as all belonging to a single general class involves taking a potentially controversial position. In the case of turbulence, I have no desire of any kind to spill coffee on you; I am simply a projectile. In the case of brainwashing, I may have a desire to steal your money and take it to my leader, but this is placed in me by the manipulations of the cult leader. We can assume that I would never have had such a desire without his intervention, and it is one which I am, by hypothesis, powerless to resist. In cases of drunkenness and stress, however, I am acting on drives and desires (unlike the turbulence case) and they seem to be internally generated (there is no cult leader or brainwasher to implant them). More explanation is therefore needed for why these kinds of cases should be taken to be similarly unrepresentative of who I am.

One reason we might think this is because we note that the behaviors we are seeing in cases of drunkenness or stress are uncharacteristic. This is someone who just does not dance on bars, or tell off her boss, or snap at her children. We have never seen her act like this except under these unusual circumstances of chemical impairment or stress. If this is what is behind our judgment, we need to consider why the fact that these behaviors are uncharacteristic should mean they do not represent the true self. One answer is simply statistical. If we think that a person's identity is what she chooses, we might conclude that the choices she makes most often tell us who she is, and that choices that are rare can be discounted in the way that one or two errant data points might be discounted in a scientific study.

This is not an entirely implausible suggestion, but there is reason to think it cannot be the whole story. If my friend escapes from the cult that has been controlling her and goes into therapy to determine why she was vulnerable to the cult in the first place, she may take hold of her life and start acting in ways that are unlike both her behavior while in the cult and her behavior before that time. There is no reason, however, to believe that she is not being herself in this case. Indeed, we might think that she is being herself for the first time. Similarly, the addict who successfully beats her addiction and gets her life back on track may act in ways that are very different from the ways she has been acting in the throes of addiction, but again, we are likely to think, if anything, that she is finally able to be herself. Whether someone is being herself thus does not seem to turn exclusively on how often she behaves in the ways we are seeing her behave now. The relevant difference appears to be whether someone is acting on a desire she wishes to act on or of which she approves.

Return to the case of the cult leader. The reason we feel that action on an implanted desire does not express the follower's true self is twofold. First, the desire is not internally generated, but implanted. Second, it is irresistible. The cases in which we say someone is not herself when impaired are usually seen as relevantly like this case in the second respect. The person who snaps at her children when under stress does not want to snap at them; she simply cannot control herself anymore and the angry words come out. This may be less clear in the case of someone who drunkenly dances on the bar, but insofar as we think she is failing to be herself we are imagining that she is driven to act this way because her powers of judgment and self-censorship are inhibited, leaving her at the mercy of whatever random impulse she happens to experience. This way of thinking about what is truly part of the self will often, but not always, coincide with the statistical picture. Assuming that most people are not usually inebriated or under unbearable stress, the uncharacteristic behaviors will not occur often either because the person would never even experience the desire to engage in them or, if she did, would immediately suppress it as unacceptable and not to be acted upon.

In the former case, situations like drunkenness and stress begin to look like brainwashing with respect to both aspects of the desire. Not only is the person not able to resist the impulse; it is one she would not have consciously experienced but for the stress or alcohol. The latter case is in some ways murkier than the former, but it helps crystallize the picture of the true self underlying the claim that we are what we choose. It is tempting to think that if the desires someone experiences while drunk are ones she experiences often while sober but suppresses, they are a part of who she really is, which she is denying. This is the thought behind the second truism, and we will return to it later. The view of the true self as what we choose, however, is based on the idea that not every impulse or desire we experience is part of who we really are. All kinds of impulses and desires arise in us all the time, proponents of this view point out, as they do in most animals. What makes humans different from possibly all other animals, however, is that we can step back from these impulses and decide whether we wish to act on them. Someone might feel an inclination to dance on the bar but also a strong desire to maintain her dignity by sticking to the dance floor. When sober, she may reliably choose the latter option, quickly dismissing the former as a perverse inclination she does not wish to follow. Disinhibited by alcohol, however, she may lose the ability to choose in the moment and be driven by impulse, thereby failing to express her true nature.

Critical to this view is the idea that we are fundamentally moral agents. This is connected to Locke's forensic or practical view of the self insofar as it thinks about the limits of the self as connected to the limits of what we are rightly held accountable for. It takes a different approach from Locke, however, insofar as it does not set those limits at what is in our consciousness, but rather at what we actively choose. We are responsible for what we do voluntarily (e.g., throwing a cup of coffee at you when you annoy me) but not for what we do involuntarily (e.g., spilling coffee on you during unexpected turbulence), even if we are fully conscious of it. One important aspect of this overall picture is that typically when we make choices we are not just choosing this action now; we are choosing a more general principle or policy for how we want to act, and so for how (and who) we want to be. In her sober moments, my friend is choosing not only not to dance on the bar now, but not to be the kind of person who dances on bars, and when someone chooses to congratulate his self-aggrandizing colleague rather than making a snarky remark, he is choosing to be the kind of person who rises above petty annoyance and acts with grace.

The guiding intuition behind this picture of the true self is that we fail to be ourselves when we have made decisions of this kind and then find ourselves unable to live up to the principles we have chosen. If I am a recovering addict who has chosen a sober lifestyle and am devastated by the fact that, time and again, I find myself unable to keep my resolution, I am not doing what *I* most want to do. I act on desires I experience, but they are not desires on which I wish to act. The same structure applies, on this view, in more ordinary and less dire circumstances of weakness of will. If I have resolved to stick to a healthy diet but find myself unable to resist eating that piece of cake, even though I know I will be miserable about it later, or if I cannot make myself sit down to work no matter how hard I try and no matter how many tips for avoiding procrastination I have implemented, I am similarly not doing what *I* want to do. The truism that people are often not themselves when inebriated or under stress thus expresses the idea that these circumstances interfere with our ability to resist impulses that undermine our choices. Our choices of principles of action are taken to determine who we truly are, and when we violate them, we are seen as not being ourselves.

Complications

There is much that is familiar and attractive in this view, but also some worries to raise about it. One is that it confuses the true self with the ideal self. The idea that our true self is determined by our choices about how we wish to act rather than the actions we take seems to imply that we truly are whoever we most want to be. As we have seen, on this view the frequency with which you act as you wish is not the relevant factor, only that this *is* how you sincerely wish to act. But what about the person who almost never acts on the principles of action that have her endorsement? If I am consistently inconsiderate to my friend, it will be a hard sell to say that because I wish I were a better friend I truly am considerate, despite my actions. What we are, it seems, cannot be so cleanly disconnected from what we do.

There are a variety of ways in which those who support the "chosen-self" view can respond to this worry. One is to clarify that if our commitments to principles of action are to constitute our identities, they must amount to more than merely thinking or saying that we want to be a certain kind of person or act on certain principles. They must be more, even, than sincerely believing this. To be committed in the relevant way someone must make a genuine effort to live up to the principles she has chosen. If my reaction to realizing I am regularly inconsiderate to my friend amounts to nothing more than vaguely wishing I were not, there is reason to wonder whether I am as committed as I say, or think, myself to be. If, on the other hand, I am mortified by my behavior and take steps to try to avoid inconsiderate action in the future, there is more reason to think that deep down I am considerate but have just had a difficult time being myself for some reason, perhaps because of stress or some other force that debilitates my strength of will.

Even where there are such efforts, however, if someone is consistently inconsiderate over time, we might wonder whether she really is committed to the principle of being considerate. I may have talked myself into believing that I am, to use a term employed by philosopher Harry Frankfurt, "wholehearted" in my decision to do better, and feel disappointed in myself when I fail to be so, but it may turn out that I am actually ambivalent (perhaps, for example, I have some unresolved anger towards this friend) and have been unable to commit fully to this value. This answer complicates the simple idea that we constitute ourselves by making wholehearted choices about which principles of action we wish to follow. Cases like this reveal that it is not easy to give a clear understanding of what such a choice entails. It cannot be that we must *always* act on a decision for it to count as wholehearted, since our starting point was the fact that sometimes we fail to do what we most want to do and so do not express our true selves in action. Wholehearted choice also cannot consist solely in our feeling settled about what we most want to do, because we have just seen that sometimes we can be self-deceived and think we are wholehearted when we are not. To have a clear sense of what it means to define the self in terms of commitment to principles of action, we thus need a more precise statement of when such a commitment has been made.

A related concern is that there seem to be cases where someone has made a wholehearted decision to act according to a principle and is able to do so, but her actions appear to suppress rather than express her true self. A clear, if somewhat cartoonish example of such a case might involve a 1950s American housewife, call her Jane, who is appalled by her impulse to study mathematics. We can imagine that this impulse is powerful and persistent. Since she was "raised right," however, she rejects it as unseemly and unfeminine, and commits to fighting the temptation to pursue a mathematical education. From time to time she finds it difficult to resist the impulse to take courses at the local college, which would require leaving her children with a babysitter and cooking a substandard dinner. Through strength of will and with the help of sedatives, however, she is mostly able to stick to her chosen principles and keep these rogue impulses at bay.

We do not tend to see such cases as triumphs of the true self over interfering drives. We are more likely to judge that Jane's love of mathematics is part of who she really is, and that social pressures have caused her to suppress her nature and live a life that does not represent her true self. This example is, admittedly, oversimplified and dated, but the core idea is familiar and realistic. We see countless examples of this general dynamic in everyday life. It is common to talk about people who do not express who they really are, do not even acknowledge it to themselves, because some feature of their identity is deemed personally or socially unacceptable. Such people may have made a clear decision not to act on these impulses, and be extremely good at controlling them, but in these kinds of cases it does not seem as if this is enough to make what they choose representative of who they really are.

There are several things, I think, driving our response to this case. Here I mention two. One is the extreme effort it takes Jane to suppress her desire to study mathematics, and the emotional toll it extracts. Her depression and need for sedatives appear as indicators that she is not living the life she truly wants to live. Another factor is discomfort with the process by which she has chosen her principles of action. The way the case is presented, we suspect that Jane is making her decision under intense social pressure, and perhaps with limited information about her options or resources to explore them. These circumstances, we may think, interfere with the ability to truly make a choice about what she wants to do. On this understanding, Jane's case is a more subtle variant on the brainwashed cult member.

Defenders of the view of the self as constituted by choice have responses to both worries. To the first, they might point out that doing what we most want to do frequently takes effort and can be very difficult. An opioid addict struggling against addiction may well go through agony and, like Jane, need sedatives and other medications to stick to her resolution. To the extent that we think an addict is acting to express rather than suppress her true self in working to overcome her addiction, the fact that it is a struggle for the housewife to keep her commitments does not by itself show that these commitments fail to represent the true self.

As for the circumstances being oppressive or coercive, defenders of the chosen-self view have two moves they can make. One is to bite the bullet and say that if this is what Jane has decisively chosen to do, then it represents who she truly is. That we do not think that the way she has resolved her conflict between studying mathematics and full-time homemaking is the best resolution does not mean that it does not represent what Jane most wants to do given the realities of her circumstances. If we do think that coercive social forces really act like addiction or brainwashing, however, defenders of the view can allow that insofar as these forces prevent Jane from being able to actually make a choice, her actions do not represent her true self. This does not mean that the true self is not constituted by our choices, however, only that in some conditions we are not able to make self-constituting choices. This is a promising response, but it requires an account of what circumstances are needed for the right kind of choice, and this turns out to be extraordinarily difficult to provide. We have a strong sense that how someone comes to have a trait or belief is deeply relevant to whether it is truly theirs, and understanding this is important to understanding the self. It is not immediately obvious, however, how to distinguish between the circumstances of choice that define identity and those that impede it.

The two challenges we have considered to the view of the self as defined by our choices in some ways rest on opposite concerns. The challenge raised by the inconsiderate friend stems from the fact that we may not be able to act as we have chosen, while the challenge raised by Jane is connected to the fact that we may conform to our choices too rigidly. Viewed another way, however, the examples we looked at make the same point, that our choices alone do not plausibly determine who we truly are. To know that we need to look also at what we do (can we, for the most part, act as we choose?) and how we feel (how great a struggle is it to do so?). This points us in the direction of the second truism.

Self-discovery

The idea that we need to look at what someone does or how she feels to know who she truly is suggests that there are pre-existing facts about the true self, independent of our choices, which can be discerned if we pay attention. This is the assumption behind the thought that people reveal their true selves when they are stressed or disinhibited. The suggestion is that people often suppress their true desires and impulses, and so fail to show their true natures in their chosen actions. If drink or stress impairs someone's capacity for self-censorship, however, he may be unable to keep these innate desires from expressing themselves in action, and we get a glimpse of his true self. The idea that we have a given nature that makes us who we truly are is an extremely common one, ubiquitous in philosophy, psychology, literature, and daily life. So, also, is the idea that someone's true nature may fail to be expressed in how he lives and that it may be unknown even to the person himself. According to this tradition, I cannot simply choose who I am; I must find it out.

This picture of the true self also faces challenges. One is to provide a more precise rendering of what constitutes one's given nature. There are a host of questions here: Am I born with my nature or is it something I develop over time? How specific is it? Is my inborn nature a set of broad tendencies and talents or something more specific? Can someone be born to be a physician or opera singer or to live in the city? It is not plausible that each of us is born with a detailed template for how to live or with a highly specific set of beliefs or values. This leaves us with a question about what kinds of features define the true self.

A related challenge is to provide an account of how we know which of a person's persistent and powerful urges express her true self. We noted earlier that Jane's case has a structure almost exactly parallel to that of the opioid addict struggling against her addiction. If we want to say that the desire to do mathematics represents Jane's true self but the desire of the opioid addict to take drugs does not represent hers, we need an explanation of the relevant difference between the cases. The strategy of pointing to the circumstances surrounding Jane's and the addict's relation to their desires seems promising here. Jane's drive to study mathematics, we might say, is a spontaneous impulse, while the addict is driven by a biochemical process whose etiology can be traced back, for instance, to the time she was prescribed painkillers for a back injury. This does seem an important and obvious difference, but it is not trivial to give a general account of what it is for a desire to be "spontaneous" in the relevant sense. It certainly cannot mean occurring without any external influences. Pursuits at the level of studying mathematics do not occur without social influences. Minimally, Jane had to be introduced to the fact that this subject exists and there has to be some infrastructure for studying it. Perhaps, moreover, she would never have wanted to study mathematics without the encouragement of a friend or mentor. The fact that social influences play a role in the development of traits and intentions does not itself seem to interfere with their being authentic to the true self. The relevant difference seems instead to be whether those social forces act for or against the person's intrinsic inclinations. The influences that discourage Jane from studying mathematics, we tend to think, are coercive, causing her to suppress what she really wants to do. Those of the well-meaning friend or mentor, by contrast, support and nurture her true inclinations.

Seeing the question of whether socially influenced behavior suppresses the true self or facilitates its expression as turning on whether they flow from coercive or supportive influences seems like the right idea. The problem is that if we do not already have an independent way to know which inclinations represent the true self, it is not obvious how to know which kinds of influences are which. To those who take it for granted that women should have the same opportunities as men, supporting Jane's desire to study mathematics will appear to nurture her true self. To Jane's conservative family, however, it may look quite otherwise. They might see themselves as encouraging her to develop her true nature as a woman and those who support her attempts to study mathematics as freethinkers with loose values who are brainwashing and confusing her. They would view their attempts to keep her focused on her wifely duties as akin to the addict's family helping her to stay strong despite friends who are trying to lure her back to the addictive lifestyle after she is sober. Such differences in viewpoint are not an abstract possibility; they are visible throughout our social world every day (consider, for instance, debates about providing gender-affirming care for minors).

We might think that the failure of this approach to provide a clear picture of the true self shows that it is a mistake to try to make the distinction between inclinations that are truly ours and those that are not in terms of the kinds of social influences that encourage them. We might focus instead, for instance, on the effects of acting on these inclinations. Views of the true self as something to be discovered often suggest that discovering and expressing one's true self is essential to living a full and happy life. On this account, we can tell that Jane's desire to do mathematics is part of her true self if studying brings her joy and causes her to flourish. This approach appears to allow us to draw a distinction between Jane's pursuit of mathematics and the addict's pursuit of drugs, even though there are some structural similarities between these cases. While the addict may find immediate relief and even a sense of joy in taking opioids, ultimately this behavior will lead to illness and death. Freeing herself from her addiction, we think, will lead to a happier and more fulfilling life. Jane, by contrast, can be expected to feel increasing satisfaction in her study of mathematics, and increasing frustration if she suppresses it.

This approach is related to the common idea that we know we are expressing our true selves when what we do "feels right." When we stop fighting who we are and live as our true selves, what had been a demoralizing struggle becomes light and easy; we are energized and joyful, comfortable in our own skins and excited to live our lives. Something sounds right about this approach. When we find a career or place to live that seems like a perfect fit it feels like this is what we were meant to do or where we were meant to be; that we are recognizing who we truly are and how we were meant to live.

Trying to turn this feeling into a fully developed method for distinguishing between traits and inclinations that are part of the true self and those that are not, however, faces familiar challenges. To use this method for determining what represents the true self, we need a more precise definition of what it means for someone to "flourish," which is notoriously difficult to provide. It is easy to tell the difference between Jane becoming a successful mathematician who is deliriously happy and an addict spiraling into illness and despair. Things are rarely so clear-cut, however. The social factors that oppose Jane are still going to be in place if she decides to study mathematics. She may thus experience a great deal of frustration in trying to pursue her interest in mathematics, as well as financial and other stresses. She may be cut off from her husband, children, and friends. It is not likely, moreover, that nothing in her housewifely life expressed anything about Jane's true self, and so what she experiences as a mathematician may not be unmitigated joy. Neither lives nor people are so simple that we can count on there being a clean and obvious distinction between a life that expresses the true self and one that does not, or between a flourishing life of true self-expression and a dismal life of self-suppression.

There are, moreover, questions about whether we can always take a sense of rightness or joy as a sure sign that what we are doing expresses who we truly are. To begin, we need to ask what timescale we must consider in determining how to interpret the effects of acting on a particular inclination. We have already noted that the addict may feel a short-term sense of rightness and relief upon taking drugs; the problems show up only over time. By the same token, a change of jobs or relationships might be attended with an intense sense of relief, excitement, and purpose, leading someone to conclude that they have finally found what they were meant to do or the person they were meant to be with. Often, however, the relief and excitement turn out to stem mostly from the novelty of the new circumstance and the possibilities inherent in a fresh start. As the inevitable stresses, conflicts, and compromises that are part of long-term jobs and relationships accumulate, the new circumstance may feel no more self-expressive or right than the last.

The concept of flourishing is, moreover, subject to the same kinds of interpretive disagreements as the idea of oppressive social forces. Since it is not realistic to envision the relevant form of flourishing as an immediate, complete, and lasting sense of peace and joy, there is room to argue whether the effects of following a particular inclination are an example of it. If someone joins a fringe religious or political group, for instance, she might experience a euphoria or sense of purpose that feels to her as if she has found her true self, while to her family it may appear that she has been brainwashed and separated from everything she really cares about. Given the complexities of identifying the appropriate notion of flourishing, this approach leaves us again without a straightforward way of determining whether an element is part of the true self.

There is a different kind of approach to understanding the true self that might seem a promising route to mitigating these uncertainties, but in fact ends up in the same place. Jane's family

48

might object that her desire to abandon her duties to her children in order to study mathematics is "unnatural." This might mean only that they feel it is not natural to Jane, which is the question we have been considering, but they might also mean that it is not natural to beings of Jane's kind, in this case women. So far, we have been thinking of the true self in terms of an individual nature, but many believe that there is also a fundamental human nature. While there may also be additional features specific to an individual self, according to this approach an individual cannot be who she truly is without expressing her more general nature as well. Being your true self on this view is not (or not only) expressing what is uniquely you, but rather being an excellent example of your general kind, what beings like you were meant to be.

An example of this idea can be found, for instance, in religious beliefs that humans are made in the image of a benevolent God, and that actions that express the divinity infused in our nature reveal the true self, while bad actions are deviations or distortions of that nature. As it turns out, there is robust data from social science research indicating that the view of the true self as the morally best self runs deep. Given scenarios where someone resolves to do something morally good but can't bring himself to do it, study participants overwhelmingly judge that the person depicted is weak of will and has failed to act on their true desires. Given scenarios where someone resolves to do something bad and can't bring himself to do it, by contrast, participants mostly judge that the true self has broken through the fog of confused bad intentions, and the action shows us who the person really is deep down. This and similar asymmetries of judgment have been found repeatedly, among a variety of populations.

The picture of the true self as the morally best self undoubtedly represents one powerful strand of our thinking about the self, but it is not going to solve our problem of conflicting judgments about when an inclination or action is rightly attributed to someone's true self. That would require agreement about which actions and inclinations are morally good, and there is at least as much divergence on this point as there is on the question of which social influences are oppressive, and what constitutes flourishing. Study participants overwhelmingly agree that becoming morally better is becoming who one truly is, but whether they judge that some particular change involves expression of the true self depends upon how they (and not the person who is changing) feel about that change. Participants diverged, for instance on whether someone who had been struggling against desires for same-sex romantic involvement and finally succumbs to them has lost themself or become more fully themself. The difference correlates, unsurprisingly, with the respondent's views about the morality of same-sex relationships.

There is, moreover, another powerful strand of thought about the self that pulls in the opposite direction. The idea of human nature as fundamentally good does run deep, but so does the view of humans as fundamentally evil or amoral. This strand is displayed in well-known literary works like *Lord of the Flies* and *Heart of Darkness*, as well as the 1930s American radio show *The Shadow*, which asked what "evil lurks in the hearts of men." In philosophy, it is found, among other places, in Thomas Hobbes's famous claim that without the constraints of civil society our hostile, aggressive natures would make the lives of humans "nasty, brutish, and short." Figures like Nietzsche and Freud paint a similar picture of our inner nature and, while each acknowledges that some form of restraint is required to discipline our more destructive impulses, both also suggest that the false idea of a good nature from which we are constantly deviating is deeply destructive. We are the animals we are, they argue, and having to pretend perpetually that we do not feel the impulses natural to such animals causes confusion and self-destructive behavior.

Challenging the idea of the true self as the best self does not require dramatic examples of monsters or claims about our dark nature. Recall that while Jane presented one challenge to the chosen-self view, another came from the inconsiderate friend. The second of the two truisms with which we started is often invoked in contexts where unlovely features of the self are revealed. When inebriated or stressed, someone may reveal aggressive tendencies or vanity or a jealous, petty nature, or racism/sexism/xenophobia, and we might think, "Aha! Now I know who he really is." This does not necessarily imply that we must judge him to be fundamentally evil, only that his worse angels are as much a part of who he is as his better angels.

It turns out to be difficult to flesh out the theory of the true self behind either of the two truisms with which we started, let alone to provide decisive considerations in favor of one rather than the other. The fact that we cannot agree on a criterion for what makes a feature part of the true self does not necessarily mean that there is no such criterion, but it does raise questions about whether there might not be an understanding of the true self that does not depend upon determining a distinct set of psychological traits that defines it.

The story of my life

One of the things that makes it so difficult to settle on an account of the true self is that all the competing considerations we discussed have some plausibility in some circumstances. It does seem as if sometimes people reveal their true selves when disinhibited or impaired, but also that simply acting out whatever impulse they experience is not plausibly what it means for them to be who they truly are. Being able to endorse what we do does seem important to establishing a proper identity, but not if we ignore deep and persistent clues that we are choosing against the grain. The causes of a trait or impulse (social, physiological, or environmental) seem relevant to whether it represents the true self, as do its effects, but neither seems entirely determinative of whether it represents who someone really is. There seems to be some broad human nature, containing both moral and amoral/immoral elements, but it is hard to pin down or to know how much it might change over time. Rather than trying to decide among these elements which defines the true self, a good strategy might be to consider whether we can think about the true self in a way that has a place for all of them. On this approach, we do not expect what is part of the true self to be determined by any one factor, but rather by a complex set of factors interacting over time.

One powerful example of this approach thinks of the self in narrative terms. The idea that our lives are somehow story-like, and that we are each protagonist and author (or, more realistically, co-author) of that story is a familiar one. If I want to know someone, I want to know their story. This idea has found its way into examinations of the self in many scholarly disciplines, including philosophy, psychology, sociology, and literary theory. It takes multiple forms and has been subject to several challenges, but it offers some important resources for thinking about the self. The guiding thought is that the unity of a self can be understood through an analogy with the unity of a narrative. Narratives, like selves, are complex wholes that unfold and develop over time. There is a strong connection among the parts of a single narrative, but there is no single feature or set of features that defines it as a single, ongoing story. Its nature and unity are uncovered through attention to the ongoing dynamic interactions among its elements. The meaning, significance, and character of individual events in a narrative come from the context of the story in which they occur. A passage in a novel or scene in a film takes a great deal of its meaning from what has transpired already and what is expected to happen next. As the story continues, we often reassess our initial understanding of events in light of what happens. This sort of interpretive work is sometimes done explicitly, as when we are engaged in literary criticism, but a form of it is undertaken implicitly whenever we read a novel or watch a film and engage with it *as* a story.

The narrative approach to understanding the self suggests that we "read" selves, including our own selves, in something like the way we read stories. In living our lives, we experience what happens to us in the context of our ongoing lives, and the character of individual events depends on this context. Winning the lottery, for instance, is one thing for the struggling parent trying to feed her family and another for the mega-rich gambling addict who succumbed to temptation and bought a ticket after years of abstinence. Walking through a jetway is one experience if one is taking a much needed and well-deserved holiday, another if one is arriving for a job interview, and yet another if one is traveling to the funeral of a beloved friend. We do not have to stop and think about the context in which these events occur for these differences to be experienced. This context is always operating in the background, coloring our experience. This is also true in our assessment of other selves. In understanding others, we start with a background idea about what a human life is like in general and make preliminary assumptions about their nature based on this. The more we learn about someone's individual story and about the role of particular actions, events, or traits in their life history, the better we understand who they are. The narrative approach thus sees the self as something incredibly complex with multiple dimensions interacting in intricate ways over time.

This approach does not yield a simple "yes" or "no" answer to the question of whether a particular inclination or action is part of the true self or peripheral. Instead, it offers a nuanced picture of ways in which it does and does not express who someone truly is. If I know, for instance, that my friend is someone who tends to be inconsiderate when she is under pressure, I may understand that her lack of consideration does not mean the same thing in the context of her life that it might in a different context while also taking the fact that she has this tendency as relevant to my overall understanding of who she is. More generally, the narrative approach allows us to take account of both the background causes of actions and inclinations (What kind of social forces were active

53

in forming them? Was there a cult leader or illness involved? Intoxication? Unexpected turbulence?) and its effects (Do they lead to misery or happiness long-term? Do they cause shame or pride? Are they something the person fights or allows to happen?). This approach does not automatically allow us to resolve all the uncertainties of the other approaches, but it does allow us to include the various kinds of information these approaches take to be relevant to understanding the true self in a single view.

The narrative view of the self faces its share of serious challenges and criticisms, of course. As powerful as the fundamental idea may be, spelling out the details is not easy. Many basic questions are difficult to answer, for instance: What is a narrative? Are the narratives that make selves just like literary narratives or are they different? If different, how? Who tells the self-narrative and in what circumstances? The same events can be narrated in multiple different ways. If my self-narrative differs from the story of my life others tell, or from the one I told before, how do we know which is correct? Different narrative theorists answer these specific questions in different ways, leading to further refinements and challenges.

There are also concerns about thinking of our lives and selves in narrative terms that apply to most or all specific versions of this approach. Human lives, it is argued, do not have the shape and characteristics of narratives. Literary narratives are carefully crafted artifacts. They have a beginning, middle, and end in a sense that lives do not. Works of literature, unlike human lives, contain themes and purposes, and the elements within them are carefully chosen to express those themes and further those purposes. Life, by contrast, is full of mundane activities and accidental events. To think of our lives as narratives, it is thus argued, is necessarily to fictionalize and distort them. The narrative theorist can respond to many of these worries, but it is undeniable that narratives, even nonfiction narratives, are by nature selective in what they include. This selection is typically undertaken in a way that emphasizes themes or patterns the author wishes to draw out. Critics thus worry that thinking of ourselves in narrative terms is an invitation to self-deception, while thinking of others in this way presents a powerful danger of oppression. This is especially so when family or societal narratives constrain someone's self-understanding (as, e.g., in the case of Jane). While there are some ways to mitigate these dangers, they are real.

In assessing the narrative view of the true self, we need to distinguish among three questions. One is whether we do form and understand selves through a narrative lens, another is whether doing so is necessary to developing a true self, and a third is whether this is overall a good thing to do so. The structure of these questions is interestingly reminiscent of those raised about the value and existence of the metaphysical self at the end of the first chapter when assessing the no-self view. There are reasons to think that self-narratives, at least, can be distorting, but if we do or must understand ourselves in narrative terms, it is a good idea to have a clear picture of the powerful influence of narrative thinking and the kinds of distortions to which we are prey. The narrative approach is thus a powerful tool for understanding the true self and, as we will see in the next chapter, the self more generally. We should, however, be mindful of its limitations.

Chapter 4
Waxing and waning selves

The Lockean idea of the self with which we started sees selves as psychologically sophisticated, self-conscious subjects of experience, aware of their own continuation over time. Humans do not start out with the cognitive and emotional capacities required to be such selves, however, nor do they necessarily retain these capacities throughout their biological lives. Some humans, moreover, never acquire them. To understand the nature of the self it is thus important to consider what to say about humans (and nonhumans) who do not meet the Lockean criteria for selfhood. Doing so is not only instructive in its own right but can also contribute to our ongoing reflections concerning the relationship between basic continuity of consciousness and other forms of continuity associated with the continuation of the self.

Where do selves come from? Where do they go?

Infants clearly do not meet the requirements for being Lockean selves, but in the typical course of human development, they come to do so. In thinking about what to say about the selfhood of infants and other humans who are not Lockean selves, it will be instructive to consider how this transition occurs. The most detailed discussion of this process is found in developmental psychology. Work in this area has discovered that infants are more psychologically complex at birth than once thought. Early infancy is not the "blooming, buzzing confusion" once described by William James, but involves a great deal of cognitive structure from birth. Nevertheless, very young infants are not yet capable of the kind of reason and reflection that makes them appropriate targets of moral praise and blame, and so not yet Lockean selves. The field of developmental psychology is vast and varied, offering many diverse accounts of how infants become such selves, but there is widespread agreement about certain milestones. The emergence of a mature self is typically connected to the development of a sense of self associated with a cluster of cognitive developments over the first four or five years of life. Among these are self-recognition, the ability to distinguish between one's own beliefs and those of others, and awareness of oneself as continuing over time.

Self-recognition develops with the ability to identify images of oneself *as* representations of oneself. This signals an awareness of the subjectively experienced self as an object for others, and in humans usually appears in the second year of life. A classic test to demonstrate the presence of self-recognition involves placing a sticker on the forehead of a child who is sleeping. When the child wakes up, she is shown her reflection in the mirror. If she touches the marking on her own head or pulls off the sticker, this is taken to show that she recognizes the image in the mirror as an image of her own body, something she also experiences internally. She is not just looking at *someone* with a sticker on her head, but at *herself*, seen from another perspective. The forehead in the mirror is the same one that she can reach up to touch. It is worth mentioning that this is a test that several nonhuman animals are also able to pass, a point whose implications we will consider later.

The ability to distinguish between one's own beliefs and those of others is tested by having children witness a scenario in which two people are in a room containing some desirable object (e.g., a bar of chocolate). The child observes the characters jointly stow the object in a secure location (e.g., a drawer). One of the characters leaves the room and the other, in sight of the child, moves the object to a new location (e.g., a box). When the first character re-enters the room, the child is asked where they will look for the object. Before approximately 4 years of age, children tend to say that the character who has re-entered the room will look for the object in its present location (the box), even though the character has no obvious way of knowing that it was moved in their absence. Starting at around age 4, however, children respond that the character will look for the object in the last location that the character (not the child) saw it. This is interpreted to show that before approximately age 4, children have not yet grasped that the knowledge and thoughts of others might be different from their own. Older children, however, are taken to have developed a recognition of others as having their own inner lives. Children also, around this age, learn to recognize themselves over time, as indicated, for instance, by the ability to identify themselves in photographs and videos of an earlier time.

There is some controversy about the design of each of these tests, as well as about how to interpret them, and so some disagreement about the precise age at which specific cognitive skills emerge. There is, however, a good deal of consensus about the basic developmental steps. Over the life course, the basic sense of self that emerges in the first few years develops in multiple ways, and new cognitive skills are added to those that establish the basic sense of self. Self-recognition develops into a self-concept which involves a sense of not just which being one is, but of what one is like. This moves from concrete traits ("I am tall"; "I have brown eyes") to more complex ones ("I am good at math"; "I am bad at sports"; "I am a good big sister") to the kinds of full-blown conceptions of self we see in adults, which were the focus of the previous chapter. The recognition of the distinction between self and other, and the ability to reason about what others are thinking and feeling from their circumstances and behavior continues to evolve, along with a more complex understanding of oneself as an object for others. The sense of oneself in time also becomes fuller and more extended, allowing for long-range planning, delay of gratification, and a long-term life plan that is organized around goals and commitments.

There are multiple approaches to the development of personality and sense of self, with further subdivisions within general approaches. Even the taxonomy of approaches is a matter of some contention. The basic format, however, is to identify life stages characterized by specific activities, capabilities, conflicts, and needs, which are associated with the different aspects of the emerging sense of self described above. Successful negotiation of each stage leads to the next, with increasing depth and sophistication of personality, culminating in the development of a mature self. Freud and neo-Freudians define this development in psychosexual terms, with different developmental stages defined in terms of a dominant erogenous zone. Erik Erikson, from whom we get the idea of an "identity crisis," offers a psychosocial account that focuses on the ways our achievement of competence and interactions with others shape our personality. Jean Piaget focuses on stages of cognitive development and the ways in which we grow in our ability to conceptualize the world. This Piagetian approach is developed further by Lawrence Kohlberg, who defines stages of moral development over the lifespan. Kohlberg's view has in turn been challenged from a feminist perspective by Carol Gilligan, reminding us of the need to account for the diversity of human experience in exploring the stages of development. Humanistic approaches such as those offered by Abraham Maslow and Carl Rogers focus on development as a drive towards self-actualization. New technologies for studying brain development have added insights from neuroscience, further refining our understanding of the stages of development and when and how they occur.

One exciting point of convergence between philosophy and psychology on these questions is around the narrative conception

Waxing and waning selves

of self, which has been popular in both disciplines. Narrative theorists in developmental psychology link the emergence of the key features of a sense of self to the acquisition of the capacity for narrative thought during the preschool years. Caregivers support the emergence of this ability by regularly telling children rudimentary stories about themselves, and so helping them to organize their experiences in a story-like form. This is a matter of prompting and response: "Where did we go today?" "To the park," "Was it fun?" "Really fun," "Who did we see there?" "Elijah," "And you and Elijah had a fight, right?" "Yeah," "And then we had to come home." "Yeah," "Then how did you feel?" "Sad," "How did Elijah feel?" "He cried," "And what are you going to do when we see Elijah tomorrow?" "Say 'sorry.'" There is a lot already going on here. The child is being prompted to understand himself as continuing over time, to connect past actions with consequences for the present and plans for further action, to relate events and actions to associated emotions, and to think about the emotions of others.

As children get older these rudimentary stories become more complex and extend further in time. Children are prompted to think about developmental milestones in the future—going to school, getting married, having children, having a career—as well as about their further past. In this way, they are exposed repeatedly to their culture's conception of the basic contours of a human life and helped to understand themselves as individuals living such lives. Eventually this self-understanding becomes individualized. If all goes well, it grows into a complex life narrative that involves goals, abilities, beliefs, and other traits peculiar to the individual. Many narrative theorists in personality psychology connect the mature self to an internalized life story organized by fundamental life goals.

In addition to connecting the psychological and philosophical discussions, the narrative view of self-development highlights the critical role of others in the development of the self, a feature we have already discussed, and which is found in almost every theory of human development. Most accounts stress the importance of a social context in which the cognitive development of the infant is supported or "scaffolded" by caregivers and, eventually, peers and a larger social network. While different accounts vary widely with respect to the degree and kind of social support they see as necessary to human development, it is generally acknowledged that without the right kinds of social interactions the capacities associated with the Lockean self will not develop in their typical form. Research has shown that children who are neglected and do not receive typical kinds of support exhibit ongoing cognitive, linguistic, and behavioral deficits. Narrative theorists have also shown that the narrative style of caregivers, and the amount of narration and storytelling to which young children are exposed, affect their developmental trajectory in predictable ways. Supporting these insights is an ever-growing understanding of the critical role responsive relationships play in brain development, especially at an early age, and hence of the ways in which lack of appropriate social interaction can alter the course of neurological development.

This extremely brief overview of the ways in which the mature, Lockean self develops is instructive because it reveals in somewhat more detail some of the main components of such selves, while reminding us that their appearance in human life is gradual, occurring in stages. It is important to recognize that these capacities can also be lost, gradually or suddenly, through a variety of accidents and illnesses, or just by aging. The paths to losing these capacities are more multifarious than the path to acquiring them, so there is not a standard trajectory to describe concerning the loss of capacities as there is generally assumed to be for their acquisition. Some of the more common ways in which this happens are, however, sadly familiar. A devastating stroke causing profound brain damage may leave someone in a minimally conscious state. Dementia, in its late stages, might leave someone conscious, but without the capacity for reason and reflection or reflexive self-consciousness that characterize selves according to Locke.

Humans, then, always start out without the sophisticated cognitive capacities in terms of which Locke defines the self, and they can also live some portion of their later lives without them. Some humans, moreover, have congenital anomalies or early brain injuries that lead to severe cognitive disabilities. They never gain these capacities, and so are never selves as Locke defines them. This leaves us with a question about what to say about humans without these capacities. Are they different kinds of selves? Are they not selves at all? If so, what are the moral and metaphysical implications?

Human nonpersons

The traditional psychological theories described in Chapter 1, having explicitly adopted a Lockean understanding of the self, seem committed to the view that infants and those in a minimally conscious state, in late-stage dementia, or with profound cognitive deficits do not meet the relevant criteria. In some sense they are willing to accept this, but there is an important and consequential complication in the way they do so. Locke, we have seen, says that "person" and "self" are names for the same thing. For him, persons are selves seen from the outside. In 20th-century versions of the psychological approach, however, the language of "self" mostly drops out in favor of the language of "person." Psychological theorists do not explicitly signal a departure from Locke on this point, but some of what they say suggests that this implies a substantive change from Locke's view and not just a terminological one. Present-day followers of Locke are unlikely to say that infants, dementia patients, and the severely cognitively disabled are not selves, but they will say, explicitly, that they are not yet (no longer, not) persons.

On first hearing, this is a rather shocking claim with potentially worrisome ethical implications. Psychological theorists can mitigate these worries to some extent by clarifying that "person" here is used as a technical, philosophical term to refer to beings who are rational agents and so can be held morally accountable for their actions. Denying personhood to some humans, they can argue, is protective rather than punitive, since it guarantees that those who are not able to truly choose their actions are not punished for them. In this "forensic" sense, nonhuman entities like corporations, for instance, can be designated persons, precisely so that they can be prosecuted for wrongdoing. The claim that some humans are not persons sounds frightening, proponents of this way of thinking explain, because we are used to connecting personhood with the right to an elevated moral status and respect. This status can be accorded to human nonpersons, however, just in virtue of their humanity. All humans, we can insist, deserve respect and moral, compassionate treatment. The point is only that those who are also persons, with the sophisticated cognitive abilities that implies, have special obligations and perhaps additional privileges.

This response is sound as far as it goes but is unlikely to do much to address the worries of those who have a loved one with dementia or severe cognitive impairment who will (in my opinion, rightly) suggest that in everyday speech labeling someone a nonperson is an insult and implies that they are not entitled to the same level of moral consideration and social standing as those considered persons. Moreover, it is not at all clear that we typically think of infants, dementia patients, and those with cognitive impairments as nonpersons. The language and application of concepts here is at best murky. Philosophers can, of course, define a technical use of "person" and draw its consequences as they please, and it can be useful to do so. Insofar as those defending Lockean views are attempting to provide a more rigorous understanding of our everyday concept of persons, though, they will need to address the counterintuitive consequences of labeling humans without the Lockean capacities "nonpersons."

However these issues are resolved, they do not yet tell us anything concrete about the *selfhood* of those who lack these capacities. The strategy described above seems to imply that these theorists are drawing a distinction between persons and selves that is not present in Locke's own view. There are reasons for wanting to make such a distinction. Because personhood is something attributed from a third-person, social perspective, it can be plausible to say that it is determined by publicly observable capacities or a role in transactions with others. Since selfhood is usually associated with subjectivity, however, and so determined from the first-person perspective, many argue that it must be understood in terms of the character of experience. It is telling that the problem cases for the Lockean definition of self involve humans who have conscious experience but lack sophisticated cognitive capacities. It seems strange to say that infants, those with dementia, and the cognitively disabled are not selves in a way that it does not seem strange to say this about very early-stage embryos or humans who have suffered irreversible brain death. This suggests that there is a way of being a self that is rooted in subjectivity but is more fundamental than the one Locke describes. The nature of this more fundamental type of self, and its connection to the basic continuity of consciousness we have been discussing, is worth exploring.

Minimal selves

There is an important strand of philosophical thought about the self that sees it as a bare subject of experience. To be a self, on this view, is just to be sentient and so to feel pleasure or pain and to have conscious experience of the world around you. Philosopher Dan Zahavi, for instance, invokes the phenomenological tradition, which investigates the structure of conscious experience and considers what it implies about self and world. Among other things, phenomenologists argue that conscious experience of any sort implies the existence of a subject whose experience it is, a "minimal" self or subject of experience. The idea of an experience without a subject to experience it, phenomenologists argue, is incoherent. There are no ownerless pains, pleasures, perceptions, or thoughts. The minimal self that serves as the subject of experience does not need reflective self-awareness or the capacity for rational thought, only consciousness and the capacity to have experience. This kind of self is found not only in infants, late-stage dementia patients, and the severely cognitively disabled, but also in any sentient nonhuman animal. It is a form of selfhood that we presumably share with dogs and cats and parrots and mice. Selves of this sort can sometimes acquire sophisticated cognitive capacities and so become persons (as most humans do), but, on this view, not every self is also a Lockean person.

We might think about the distinction between personhood and selfhood being drawn here in this way: The distinction between self and nonself allows us to capture the difference between conscious beings, capable of pain, pleasure, fear, surprise, thirst, hunger, and so on, and nonconscious things like rocks and tables. The distinction between person and nonperson, on the other hand, is meant to capture what distinguishes (most) humans from (at least most) other animals. A self, human or otherwise, is understood as a very basic kind of experiencing subject. A person, by contrast, is a being with reason, reflection, self-consciousness, and the other sophisticated cognitive capacities that are typical of mature humans. Distinguishing between persons and selves in this way has some advantages. It allows us to capture both the continuities and discontinuities between humans and other animals (we are all selves, but not all of us are persons), as well as those within the life of a developing human (it is a self for its whole life, and a person for part of it). It also provides a systematic way of explaining the moral significance of being a self of any kind. Insofar as a being is capable of experiencing pain or pleasure, it has an interest in experiencing the latter rather than the former. At the same time, it clarifies the grounds for whatever special moral obligations or privileges might apply to those who are also persons.

This distinction also raises a question. Humans tend to be both persons and selves. So, how are we to think about the relation between selfhood and personhood in a typical human? Zahavi sees minimal selfhood as basic, understanding the attributes and cognitive capacities that make us persons as embellishments of the minimal self. In its essential nature, a human self is just the same as a mouse self, a parrot self, a self with advanced dementia, or an infant self. Different selves can have different attributes and cognitive capacities, and this can make them importantly different, according to Zahavi, but none of this changes the fundamental nature of what they are. At bottom, a human self is just, like any other self, a bare subject of experience.

Zahavi develops his view in a quite different context from that in which the psychological accounts of identity discussed in Chapter 1 were developed and therefore does not say much about what is required for the continuation of a minimal self. If we consider this question, however, we will find interesting points of contact between the two discussions. Since the minimal self is understood as a bare subject of experience, it is natural to think of the persistence of such a self as consisting in the basic continuity of consciousness discussed in earlier chapters. Read this way, the general picture would be that a human life starts with a minimal self that, in typical cases, develops new attributes as it matures and may later lose those attributes through accident or illness. Importantly, though, the same minimal self is present throughout a human life on this account, and does not alter its basic nature, despite dramatic gain and loss of cognitive capacities and other features. The minimal self is seen as analogous to a room which starts out with a few sticks of simple furniture, is gradually filled with luxurious furnishings, and eventually emptied again. The room is in some ways a very different place when furnished, and it is possible to do things in the furnished room that you could not do in the empty room (hold a state dinner, for instance). Nevertheless, in a fundamental sense the room itself, the space enclosed by those four walls, has persisted unchanged all along.

Similarly, the analogy goes, the minimal self can be psychologically fancied up in multiple ways, and this may have many practical implications, but it does not change its fundamental nature.

This view is very like the view considered in Chapter 1, that the metaphysical continuity of the self is determined by basic continuity of consciousness and that changes in the contents of consciousness do not alter the fundamental nature of the self. In Chapter 2, we considered the possibility that other factors (i.e., continuity of activities and relationships) might be part of what constitutes the literal continuity of the self and suggested that they might even play a role in maintaining basic continuity of consciousness. Revisiting these issues in the context of the current discussion allows us to build on these earlier suggestions. To see how, we can consider whether we must accept the claim that the fundamental nature of the minimal self remains unchanged by cognitive development. We might instead suggest that there are different *kinds* of selves, with varying levels of complexity. Minimal selves are one type. As minimal selves develop more capacities and complexity, on this alternative view, they become different in kind and not just in character. They are still experiencing subjects, but they are different *kinds* of experiencing subject. Amoebae and humans are both organisms, and there are important similarities between them. But a human is not just an amoeba with some extra features; it is an importantly different kind of organism. The corresponding idea with respect to selves would thus be that while, for instance, mouse selves and human selves might both properly be called selves, they are selves of importantly different kinds.

If we are thinking of selves as subjects of experience, the difference in kind will have to be an experiential difference; the kind of experience had by typical mature human selves should thus be different from that had by the typical mouse self. This seems plausible, but it leaves us with the question raised earlier in the chapter about what to say about the endpoints of human life. Since a human infant, for instance, does not have the complex kind of experience characteristic of a typical mature human self, it seems it must be a different kind of self. Does that mean that the infant cannot be the same self as the mature human? This is a difficult question, but insights gained in this chapter and the last point to a promising approach to addressing it. In Chapter 3, we suggested that understanding the true self requires us to consider the origins and trajectories of someone's traits, desires, and choices. In this chapter, we have seen that the complex adult self does not come into existence all at once but emerges gradually over time. This suggests we should expand the insight of Chapter 3 beyond the true self to the self more generally. We have seen that the seeds of the complex abilities of the mature human self are present in the human infant self in a way that they are not, for instance, in a typical infant mouse self. Looking just at a moment of experience of an infant self and then at a moment of experience of an adult self, they seem to be very different kinds of selves. If we think of selves as inherently diachronic beings, however, which must be understood over time, things look different. A human self has one kind of typical developmental trajectory and a mouse self another. If we look at selves from the developmental perspective, it is thus easy to see how a human infant can be (an early) part of the same self as a mature human.

In Chapter 3, this diachronic view of the true self was connected to the concept of narrative. Earlier in this chapter we saw that this concept has also been applied to human psychological development. In developmental psychology, the narrative approach has been associated with the claim that as children learn to think of their lives in narrative terms their experience of themselves in time alters and expands. In coming to understand our present as flowing from our past and affecting our future, according to this claim, we also come to have a broader time horizon. Just as by stepping back from a painting we can include more of it in our visual field, so by taking a longer view of our lives, we can alter the range of time we directly experience. The mature adult can experience guilt and pride, anxiety and delighted anticipation, and these experiences bring the past and future experientially into the present in a way that does not happen for purely minimal selves.

Psychologists Katherine Nelson and Robyn Fivush, who have been important defenders of this view, describe how "extended, subjective autobiographical consciousness" emerges over the course of human maturation through the capacity to develop increasingly complex self-narratives that integrate our experiences over time both with each other and with the social world and ongoing events. If this is right, and if we increase the complexity of our narrative self-understanding gradually, we can take a long view on the development of the human self, seeing a single, ongoing self that begins with a truncated time horizon which broadens as a more sophisticated sense of self develops. In this picture, the self is less like a static room that gains and loses furnishings and more like one that gets expanded and connected to other rooms through structural remodeling. If this is right, developing the capacity for self-narration is a critical step in generating the kind of continuity of consciousness that is often taken to define the metaphysical continuity of self, and this capacity can be added to the continuity of activities and relationships as one of the interrelated elements that potentially play a role in supporting and maintaining basic continuity of consciousness. Since the narrative that defines the true self is seen, on this view, to grow out of the one that contributes to basic continuity of consciousness, this approach also suggests interesting points of connection between the metaphysical conception of the self and more psychological and practical ones.

It is important to make clear that what I have described is meant to articulate promising ideas for further exploration. Neither the narrative view of development nor the claim that there are fundamentally different kinds of selves is by any means uncontroversial. It is also important to be explicit that saying that there are different kinds of selves does not yet say anything about whether one kind of self is more valuable or significant than another. Research on human development and animal selves is massive and changing all the time. What it does suggest, however, is that we have reason to reflect seriously on the nature and moral significance of both the differences and commonalities between human selves and other selves. While plenty of controversies remain, the material discussed in this chapter at the very least reminds us that Lockean selves do not come into existence all at once. Their appearance is gradual and piecemeal, and this is something that needs to be taken account of in any attempt to understand the self.

Chapter 5
Divided and distressed selves

Often a great deal can be learned about what something is by considering circumstances in which its functioning is disrupted. The self is no exception. There is no shortage of examples of disruptions to the self, ranging from the common and minor to the exotic and profound. This chapter looks at a handful of psychiatric and neurological cases in which selfhood appears to be compromised. These cases are chosen for the way they both illuminate and complexify the questions we have been discussing so far.

Split-brains

Split-brain cases involve patients in whom the corpus callosum is cut to alleviate medically intractable epilepsy. The corpus callosum is a bundle of more than 200 million nerve fibers connecting the two hemispheres of the cerebrum, a part of the brain involved in sensory processing, language, judgment, and reasoning, among other things. In ordinary circumstances, the connections of the corpus callosum permit rapid and direct communication between the right and left hemispheres of the cerebrum, which typically undertake different processes (hence our descriptions of people as "left-brained" or "right-brained" depending upon which set of processes seems predominant).

In some cases of severe epilepsy, the only effective treatment is corpus callosotomy, which severs these connections.

Usually, this surgery has surprisingly little effect. In experimental studies, however, it has been possible to produce intriguing results. Generally, each hemisphere receives sensory information from, and controls, the contralateral side of the body. The right hemisphere typically processes visual input from the left field of vision and receives tactile input from and controls the left side of the body, while the left hemisphere has this same relation to the right side of the body. The relevant experiments provide different sensory information to each hemisphere. Subjects may, for instance, be placed before a screen with a divider which prevents each eye from seeing the other half of the screen. This lets experimenters provide different visual input to the right and left hemispheres by projecting different images on each side of the screen. The right side (which inputs to the left hemisphere) might be left blank, for example, while the left side (which inputs to the right hemisphere) shows a picture of a fork. Participants are then asked what they see on the screen.

In most people, the left hemisphere controls language. Since what provides visual input to the left hemisphere is a blank screen, subjects in this kind of experiment typically reply that they see nothing. If they are asked to use their left hand (controlled by the right side of the body) to pick out what they saw from a collection of objects, however, they will pick out the fork but not be able to say why they did so. There have been several variations on this kind of experiment, including one in which the two hemispheres seem to play a game of 20 Questions, with the participant offering verbal guesses about what number was displayed to the right hemisphere while the left hand points up to signify that the number on the screen was higher than the guess and down to signify that it was lower. Using this method, participants are ultimately able to state accurately what number was displayed to the right hemisphere but continue to verbally report that they did not see a number displayed.

Many philosophers and neuroscientists have taken these kinds of results to show that there are two, distinct subjects of consciousness, or selves, in the patients' bodies after corpus callosotomy; the left hemisphere, which can express itself verbally and the mute right hemisphere which demonstrates its consciousness through gestures and drawings. Some reject this interpretation, however, arguing that the admittedly strange effects elicited in experimental circumstances do not show that the right hemisphere is a distinct subject of consciousness. One line of argument for rejecting the "two-selves" interpretation suggests that the right hemisphere is not conscious. It can respond to stimuli, according to this view, but this response takes place unconsciously; its actions occur in something like the way we automatically avoid obstacles while walking without consciously noticing them. It is difficult to decisively reject this proposal since the question of what is required for an action to be conscious is notoriously thorny. Still, the flexibility and context sensitivity of the behaviors that can be elicited from the right hemisphere, and their responsiveness to linguistic queries and commands, makes them seem more like the conscious actions of human agents than reflexes (think of the 20 Questions game). The only reason we have for thinking the actions of the right hemisphere are not conscious is the verbal denial of such consciousness. But this would be expected whether the actions were conscious or not, given that the left hemisphere controls speech.

A more powerful consideration against the "two-selves" interpretation is the fact that there is not much to suggest the presence of two spheres of consciousness outside of experimental settings. In everyday life, corpus callosotomy produces little, if any, noticeable effect on behavior. If the right hemisphere really is a second self, we must wonder what happens to it when the patient leaves the experimental setting and why it does not make its presence known in daily life. Does the second self emerge only during experiments, or is it always present? Even in experimental settings, moreover, the lack of integration displayed by patients is partial, applying only to responses concerning controlled sensory input. A good deal of ongoing integration is required just to keep the body present, sitting upright, and behaving normally in all other respects. In the 1984 Hollywood comedy *All of Me*, attorney Roger Cobb (Steve Martin) accidentally has the soul of Edwina Cutwater (Lily Tomlin) deposited in his body, alongside his own. A great deal of physical comedy ensues as the two selves simultaneously try to control the actions of a single body, one for instance trying to go in one direction and the other in another, leading to a great deal of flailing and tripping. While the film is fanciful (and equates selves with souls), it reminds us of what we would expect if two, independent, noncommunicating selves were controlling different halves of a single body, something quite different from what does happen in split-brain cases, even in the experimental settings.

The difficulties with both the view that there is only one self in these cases and the view that there are two has led philosopher Thomas Nagel to suggest that there is no "whole number" of minds (or subjects of experience) in split-brains. This sounds very mysterious. It can be made less so, however, if we take it not as the claim that there is some specific nonwhole number of selves present, but rather as the claim that a self can have different degrees of unity.

These cases reveal that there are multiple routes through which the right and left hemispheres communicate to coordinate information and unify experience, and that they need not all be functional to produce the behaviors and, presumably, the experience we associate with a typical human self. Outside of the experimental context, for instance, patients can move their heads, providing homogeneous visual input to each hemisphere. Both ears can pick up ambient noise. This seems sufficient to compensate for the line of communication lost through the severing of the corpus callosum. In experimental settings these mechanisms are also disabled, leading to the strange results. Other possible communicative mechanisms remain intact, however. The lower brain is not severed, and there is reason to believe that some amount of communication between hemispheres occurs there. Both hemispheres, moreover, receive proprioceptive feedback about the position and state of the body, which plausibly accounts for the differences between these actual cases and the *All of Me* scenario. Split-brain cases thus appear to be situations in which the two hemispheres remain partially, but not fully integrated.

It may seem difficult to get a sense of what experience is like for the person (or persons) in these cases, but it is not as hard as it seems. We are pretty good at multitasking and compartmentalizing and thus familiar with a certain amount of disunity in our experience. Driving my usual route home deep in conversation with my passenger, for instance, I will be conscious of the road, the other cars, and the turns I need to make, and also of the ongoing conversation. These two domains of attention may overlap very little. If a sudden anomaly requires that I give my full attention to the road, I may become fully focused on the task of driving until the danger has passed and then divide my attention once again. These everyday cases are less extreme than split-brain cases, and I do not say they are precisely the same phenomenon. They do, however, provide some access to the fact that our experience can be more or less integrated, helping us imagine how the more extreme cases could be experientially possible.

Reflection on split-brain cases yields two important lessons about the self. The first is the one we have just discussed, that the unity of the self is perhaps not a strict, all-or-nothing thing. To the extent that we cannot confidently judge there to be two selves in this case, we recognize that there may be selves that are less integrated and unified than those we typically encounter. The second is the flip side of the first. To the extent that we see split-brain cases as involving a disruption of the self, at least in experimental settings, we recognize that the kind of unity that is missing in these settings is something we take to be important to a well-functioning self. In particular, we see that in a well-functioning self, information about experience and intended action is typically available globally to the self as a whole. In the driving case, for instance, attention is divided, but each sphere is "keeping track" so that attention can be reintegrated if required. In the experimental settings, split-brain patients have some amount of information and intention divided between the hemispheres in a way that cannot be overcome (in those settings). The *All of Me* case involves a more profound and complete division. This suggests that a certain amount of compartmentalization of attention, information, and intention is compatible with being a self, but too much division will break the self apart.

Dissociative identity disorder

How much is too much? Dissociative identity disorder (DID, previously known as multiple personality disorder) may seem like a case in which compartmentalization is so profound that it breaks a single self into multiple fully distinct selves. While this judgment is more compelling in the case of DID than in the split-brain case, we will see that even here things are not so straightforward. DID has captured the popular imagination through its depiction in books and movies such as *The Three Faces of Eve*, and *Sybil*. It is defined in the latest *Diagnostic and Statistical Manual* (DSM-5) as a disorder characterized by two or more distinct personality states or an experience of possession. Typically, there is a "host" personality that identifies with the individual's given name and social identity, and one or more "alters" or "parts," alternative personality states, often possessing their own names, traits, goals, and memories. Alters can be remarkably different from one another, having not only distinct personalities, but also variations in blood pressure, visual acuity, and allergies. Different alters might speak different languages and can perceive themselves to be of different ages and genders from the host and from each other.

Hosts and alters may or may not be aware of and/or able to communicate with one another. Often the host is not directly aware of the alters but knows something is amiss because of lost time and evidence of activity for which they have no recollection, such as unexplained injuries or unfamiliar new possessions. DID is widely accepted as a particularly severe presentation of the broader category of dissociative phenomena, in which there is a "disruption in conscious awareness or sense of identity or self." The origins of DID, like other severe dissociative phenomena, are thought to lie most often in severe trauma, especially in childhood. Distancing oneself psychologically from traumatic events and the strong emotions they engender is viewed as a protective device leading, in extreme cases, to the formation of alters to deal with those emotions and events that trigger them. The exotic nature of this illness, together with a relative dearth of empirical research and its association with the "memory wars" of the 1990s has made the diagnosis somewhat controversial. There is general agreement, however, that DID is a genuine, though rare, phenomenon.

Like split-brain cases, DID has been described as involving multiple selves in a single body. Alters do seem better candidates for distinct selves than the hemispheres of split-brain patients do; they exhibit distinct personalities and goals and have individual (albeit gappy) narrative histories that do not combine easily into a single life narrative. There are, however, some compelling reasons to think of those with DID as single, fractured selves rather than multiple distinct selves. While alters possess some of the elements of full-blown selfhood, they are also generally acknowledged to differ in important ways from typical mature selves. Since alters develop to deal with specific situations or emotions, they tend to be unidimensional. Frequently, they are fragmentary and underdeveloped, and there can be a great deal of overlap among alters with respect to their traits, meaning that they are not always clearly distinguishable from one another. Usually, at least some alters can be directly aware of the thoughts and actions of the host and/or at least some other alters in the way we are typically acquainted with our own thoughts and actions, but not those of others.

Reasons for thinking of DID patients as single, fragmented selves are also found in the typical etiology and treatment of the condition. To the extent that DID is seen to result from a trauma that leads to the segmenting of memories and emotions too overwhelming to process, it seems like an extreme form of compartmentalization rather than a true generation of new selves. The standard goal of treatment, which is "integration" or "fusion," would amount to ending the existence of one or more individuals if alters were truly distinct selves. As the name implies, however, successful integration does not entail the simple elimination of all but one personality state. It instead puts the alters in communication so that they can inform and influence one another, allowing for the emergence of a single subjective sense of self that has access to the totality of memories, feelings, thoughts, and traits that had previously been distributed among the alters.

It is worth noting that there is a robust online community of "plurals," some of whom identify as having DID ("plural" is a broader category), that embrace their multiplicity, understanding themselves as "systems" of multiple "parts" or "headmates" (this sometimes involves seeing the system as many distinct selves and sometimes as one multiplicitous self). Some who identify as plurals have rejected the treatment goal of integration and instead seek functional multiplicity, and some therapists are willing to recognize this as an alternate aim. Integration is, however, a process, and after stabilizing as functional systems some patients return to pursue total integration. Moreover, many spontaneously integrate after successful treatment for other post-traumatic

The Self

symptoms, even though integration was not a specific treatment aim. There is, furthermore, some evidence that those who achieve full integration have better overall outcomes, with less depression and post-traumatic stress and fewer somatic systems than those who only partially integrate. The website of the Dissociative Identity Disorder Research Organization recognizes the complexity of these matters, and some of the genuine losses that might follow on integration, but concludes that "[H]ealthy integrations feel like what they are: an acceptance of aspects of oneself that one wasn't previously able to fully accept."

While controversy continues and there is much more to be learned about this condition, the case of DID reinforces the lessons learned in the split-brain case. It shows once again that unusual compartmentalization of experience, information, and agential intent disrupts but does not necessarily dissolve the self. In DID this disruption is much deeper and broader than in split-brain patients, yet it is still not obvious that the self has entirely disintegrated. This case offers some additional insights as well. The division of the self seems so much more profound in the case of DID not simply because information is more compartmentalized than in the split-brain case, but also because alters seem, in addition to the partial distinctness of their spheres of experience, to have different distinctive traits, goals, desires, and values. They also live somewhat separate lives with different partners, friends, hobbies, and sometimes different employment. But if these elements make the alters seem more like selves, it is at the same time their partial, unidimensional nature that makes us inclined to say that they are parts of a single individual. Because none of the alters has control of the body all the time, each is unable to pursue these activities as a unified self would. The host and alters typically cannot put together a coherent narrative of their activities because of lost time, and their emotional profile seems truncated. Our mixed feelings about the number of selves present thus reflects several aspects of the unity that we expect in a robust human self and suggests interrelations among them. The narrative and trait-related elements of self are disrupted in ways that seem connected to the global accessibility of the information about the contents of experience. Some amount of our sense of the unity of a single, disordered self undoubtedly also comes from the fact that there is only a single human body present, and it is this fact that also prevents the alters from developing into full, mature human selves by regularly interrupting their pursuits.

Affect, agency, ownership

Additional insight into the factors that make up a typical self can be found by considering disorders involving a different kind of first-personal disunity. Depersonalization/derealization disorder is one of the family of dissociative disorders to which DID also belongs but is more common and less extreme. It involves feelings of removal from oneself (depersonalization) and/or the world (derealization). Patients suffering from depersonalization feel remote from their thoughts, feelings, and actions. They complain of emotional numbness, as if they are in a "bubble" or "fog" or "wrapped in gauze." Those with this condition often also feel disconnected from their bodies. They know what is happening to them but say there is a sense in which they do not really experience it. They also lack a sense of agency with respect to their movements, frequently saying they feel like automata. It is, they say, as if they are in a dream, or under the influence of consciousness-dampening drugs. Derealization, which often co-occurs with depersonalization, is a feeling of the unreality of one's environment. Frequently patients complain that their senses seem distorted, that things look flat, or blurry, or strangely sized, or far away, or colorless. Those experiencing these states are not delusional. They are aware that these experiences are distortions and do not believe they are disconnected from their bodies, or that the world is changing shape or size. Many people have occasional episodes of depersonalization and/or derealization; the disorder is diagnosed when these episodes are continuous or extremely frequent and interfere with functioning.

This disorder does not involve any disunity in direct and immediate first-personal access to what is done or experienced, as split-brains and DID do. What is missing is the affect and sense of intimacy and agency we typically feel towards our own experiences. Those who have this disorder report that it is as if *they* are not really saying or doing these things, even though they know that they are. Although those with the disorder have difficulty explaining exactly what they are feeling, what they do say is instructive. They report basically ordinary awareness of what they see and think and do. The thoughts and sensations are in their consciousness, and they are perfectly aware of them. The strangeness of the experience comes from a lack of emotional engagement and a feeling of passivity. It is as if the experiences and actions of which they are directly conscious are observed drifting by a window rather than actively experienced or undertaken. The subjective self is there but attenuated.

This adds an important new dimension to our understanding of the nature and unity of the self. It suggests that there can be disrupted and disunified self-experience without compartmentalization of the information in consciousness. The disunity here is, roughly speaking, between the self as knower and the self as an interested and engaged agent. Of special significance is the fact that those who suffer from depersonalization/derealization disorder do not just describe this as a sense of alienation from what they experience, but as an overall dampening of consciousness. This suggests that the quality and scope of the kind of consciousness which makes up the experiencing subject or self depends not only on what one is aware of or the information to which one has access, but also on emotional and agential involvement. One is, it appears, less fully conscious without this involvement. If this is so, it raises intriguing possibilities for further connecting the idea of the self as a conscious subject of experience to the idea of the true self, which is typically understood in terms of agency and what we care most about.

These observations are developed by reflecting on the related phenomenon of "thought insertion," a symptom of schizophrenia. Individuals who have this symptom have thoughts that occur within their own consciousness but are experienced as belonging to someone else. Inserted thoughts are often connected with verbal hallucinations, another frequent symptom of schizophrenia. Some believe that these symptoms are in fact variants of the same phenomenon. Pressed for further description, patients who report verbal hallucinations often say the voices they hear do not sound like a real person talking to them but are heard inside their head "like thoughts," or at "some kind of border between thinking and hearing." Others describe their hallucinations as "like telepathy" or "almost like how telepathy would sound if it were real." As with depersonalization/derealization disorder, this case involves reports of the experience of thoughts of which a subject is directly and immediately aware as not being fully their own. The form of alienation here is somewhat more profound than in depersonalization, however. Inserted thoughts are attributed to an external source, rather than described as one's own estranged thought.

Some philosophers have analyzed inserted thoughts in terms of a distinction between "ownership" and "agency." Those who experience inserted thoughts experience them as theirs insofar as they occur in their consciousness, but as not theirs insofar as they do not experience themselves as the authors of these thoughts, reenforcing the suggestion found in our observations about depersonalization/derealization disorder that the feeling of basic "mine-ness" that attaches to states of the self does not come exclusively from the fact that we have direct and immediate awareness of them, but also from a characteristic feeling of agency and an affective response. Our thoughts and intentions are not just known to us; they seem to arise from us. And we do not just know what we experience; typically, we care about it in a particular way. The link between consciousness and concern is, you will recall, something Locke emphasized as well. When awareness is present without the typical affect and concern, what we are aware of does not feel like *our* experience. Indeed, it does not even feel as if it is fully part of our consciousness. The self can thus become disunified or disrupted not only by compartmentalization of access to information, but also when characteristic attitudes and emotions are absent from awareness.

Alienated bodies

The cases we have considered so far show some of the ways in which subjects can be alienated and disunified with respect to their subjective experience. There are also circumstances in which people become estranged from their bodies in interestingly parallel ways. A dramatic example is described by Oliver Sacks, who as a medical student was called to the hospital to deal with a patient who had fallen out of bed. The patient, who was in for neurological tests, felt fine when he went to sleep but ended up on the floor in a highly excited state in the middle of the night. On investigation the cause of his fall turned out to be the fact that he did not recognize his left leg as his own. He had awakened to find what he took to be a dead, severed leg in bed with him. He thought perhaps one of the nurses had played a trick, bringing in a cadaver leg to scare him. In trying to throw it out of his bed, he had fallen with it. When Sacks arrived, the patient still did not acknowledge the leg as his own, which he believed had disappeared. He punched it, jabbed at it, and tried to pull it off his body. The patient could see the leg perfectly well and was able to report that it was attached to his body but refused to accept it as his. Other examples of this phenomenon have since been documented.

This case again has interesting echoes of Locke's understanding of the self. While Locke insists that personal identity over time is determined by psychological factors (sameness of consciousness), he also suggests that the body with which one is associated at a given time is part of oneself because it communicates directly with one's consciousness. We experience what happens to our bodies, and so care about their condition in a very particular, first-personal way. He tells us that a person is a being "which is sensible, or conscious of Pleasure and Pain, capable of Happiness or Misery, and so is concern'd for it *self*, as far as that consciousness extends."

The limits of the self are determined by the limits of what affects our happiness or misery in this direct and immediate way. He argues that if a finger were severed from someone's body so that they no longer experienced what happened to it, it would no longer be part of their self. If somehow the consciousness went with the finger, however, so that the person experienced what happened to the finger and not what happened to the rest of the body, he says that the self would now reside entirely in the finger.

It is natural to read this claim as saying that the fact that we are conscious of what happens to a body or body part is what makes us concerned about it, and so makes it a part of what we are. We experience what happens to some particular mass of matter, and we want our experience to be pleasant rather than painful, so we care about that mass of matter; it is *our* body. The cases of depersonalization/derealization and inserted thoughts complicate this straightforward reading. These cases show that direct awareness does not automatically generate feelings of concern, and more significantly, that direct awareness without concern dampens consciousness, suggesting that concern plays a role in generating conscious awareness as well as the other way around. Self-regarding concern may thus not be just a by-product of direct awareness but seems to contribute directly to the kind of subjective experience taken by many to determine what is part of the self.

Another kind of case makes this same point in a slightly different way. Neglect Syndrome, usually occurring after a stroke or similar brain injury, is a condition in which patients have difficulty noticing or responding to stimuli on the left side of their bodies (typically the damage affects the right hemisphere of the brain). Although obviously related to split-brain cases, this is a different phenomenon. Those who have this syndrome appear not to notice objects in their left field of vision, even quite large ones (and without artificial experimental barriers). They may eat food only from the right side of a full plate and then ask for a second helping or respond to auditory or tactile stimuli only to the right side of their bodies. Inattention to the left half of one's own body, including failure to use the left limbs, is also part of this syndrome. Patients are, moreover, often unaware of this neglect. They do not complain of a constricted field of experience or paralysis.

Importantly, the neglectful behaviors are not attributable to a primary sensory or motor deficit. It is not that patients do not take in sensations from the left region of their spatial field. If directed forcefully to attend to them they can usually report what they are. Similarly, the left limbs of these patients are not paralyzed, they simply do not think to use them. In some sense, awareness of the left side of the body is intact. Uninterest and lack of reaction to what is happening there is so profound, however, that it is difficult to think of these patients as fully conscious of it. Once again, we see that our consciousness of states of the self should be understood not only in terms of direct access to information, but also as an engaged concern and sense of agency.

Reflection on some of the many ways in which the unity of self can be challenged has provided valuable insight into the complexity of typical human selves, as well as suggesting new ways in which some of the multiple conceptions of the self that we have been considering may be interdependent. We have seen that direct and immediate awareness of one's own thoughts and experiences, engagement, concern, and agential involvement are all usually a part of self-experience, and that it is in their interaction that a robust sense of a unified self emerges. We have also seen reason to believe that there are constraints on the degree to which we can make sense of multiple selves in a single body, at least in part because of the role embodiment plays in living the kind of life that allows for the relevant form of experience. In the next chapter we look at the connection between self and embodiment in more detail, as well as associated questions about social components of the self.

Chapter 6
Embodied, social selves

Attempts to define the self often begin by drawing a distinction between selves and the bodies they inhabit (as in Chapter 1) or between self and others. The need to draw these distinctions suggests that selves like us are generally encountered in embodied form, and in the company of other selves. The use of such distinctions to define the self suggests a presumption that these features are not intrinsic parts of the self and that the essential self is to be found by abstracting from them. As we have investigated different dimensions of the self, however, we have uncovered complex dynamics among self, body, and others that challenge this simple picture. This chapter considers a few of the many different direct arguments that have been given for seeing selves as essentially embodied beings, embedded in a world of objects and other selves.

Embodiment and environment

We started with the familiar idea of the self as a subject of experience. As we saw in Chapter 1, one motivation for this view is the sense that it is possible to imagine oneself outside of one's (present) body. This conception of self runs deep in the history of philosophy. We saw it in the work of Locke, and noted that it is prevalent in many religious, philosophical, and spiritual traditions which predate Locke by a long way. There are, however, views of the self that argue that we cannot understand what a self is without appreciating the conditions of its embodiment and interactions with a broader environment. These views intersect in various interesting ways with the observations made in the previous chapter about the role of affect and agency in the constitution and unity of the experiencing self.

One example of this kind of view concentrates on the way in which effective immune response depends upon the ability to discern the difference between what is internal and what external. Organisms face threats to their integrity from pathogens. To protect against these threats, most organisms possess physical barriers like skin or cell membranes, which provide a line of demarcation between organism and environment. Some pathogens, however, will make it past this barrier, and more complex organisms have ways of destroying or neutralizing such invaders. In vertebrates like humans, this is the work of the antibody-based immune system. To protect the organism without harming it, the immune system needs to distinguish between foreign substances and self. If intruders are not recognized as such, antibodies may not be mobilized to neutralize potentially harmful incursions; failure to recognize self as such can result in dangerous and disabling autoimmune conditions. Some thus argue that the very idea of a distinction between self and nonself is rooted firmly in the organism's fundamental task of self-preservation. According to this view, the first "self" is the body which is to be defended. The psychological understandings of the self we have been discussing are taken to be abstractions of this more basic sense of self, on which they are dependent.

A different way of tying the concept of self to the basic need to maintain bodily integrity focuses on neurological mechanisms for self-monitoring rather than immune response. An important version of this approach is developed by Antonio Damasio in his account of the biological underpinnings of consciousness and self. Consciousness, according to Damasio, arises from an organism's representation of itself and the world in interaction. More specifically, he offers a working definition of consciousness as a "momentary creation of neural patterns which describe a relation between the organism, on the one hand, and an object or event, on the other," adding that this "composite of neural patterns describes a state that, for lack of a better word, we call the *self*." Human consciousness involves a hierarchy of notions of the self that can be defined in terms of increasingly complex forms of inner representation and connection to consciousness issuing, ultimately, in mature human selves as we know them.

The most basic of these, the "proto-self," is not yet conscious. It is "a coherent collection of neural patterns which map, moment by moment, the state of the physical structure of the organism in its many dimensions." In addition to monitoring our inner state, humans also receive continuous sensory input from the environment, which the brain represents as images of the external world. The next stage of complexity, at which both consciousness and a sense of self first emerge, is when the organism not only represents its inner state and external objects and events, but also generates a higher-order representation of their connection, that is, of one's proto-self being affected by the processing of an external stimulus. This gives rise to a very basic awareness of *oneself* as an entity affected by objects in the world. This is, in Damasio's terminology, the development of "core consciousness" and a "core self."

Since the organism is constantly affected by its environment and the proto-self is constantly updated, the core self is also changing constantly, and must be understood as a fleeting experience of self which is basically generated anew every moment. Full-blown, enduring human selves require further cognitive apparatus, like autobiographical memory, which appears only in extremely complicated animals. This form of memory provides yet one more level of representation, allowing us to track patterns of change in response to the environment along many dimensions and at multiple levels. This allows for a form of consciousness extended over time which provides an experience of ourselves as enduring beings. Each level of awareness, Damasio says, depends on those below it. Enduring human selves are in many ways far removed from proto-selves, but they cannot exist without them.

Many of the ideas in Damasio's view are familiar from earlier discussion. The fleeting nature of the proto- and core self is connected to the neurologically based forms of the "no self" view we saw in Chapter 1. The distinction between the "core self" and the autobiographical self, both existing at the same time with the latter requiring the former, makes the former very like Zahavi's minimal self. The idea that a new level and kind of consciousness arises when these fleeting selves are connected via an autobiographical sense is reminiscent of the idea from Chapter 4 that a narrative sense of self can potentially transform a minimal self into a full-blown human self (although on Damasio's picture, the core self continues throughout, and in this respect, it is also like Zahavi's view).

A further important feature of Damasio's view, connected to our discussion in the previous chapter, is the central role it gives to affect. One of the ways traditional approaches to self and consciousness go wrong, he argues, is by assuming that experience of the self is fundamentally like experience of the external world. His account of self and self-consciousness suggests a profound and, in his opinion, underappreciated difference. The representation of our inner state, he says, always involves some experience of pleasure or pain. Like the immune system, our self-monitoring systems evolved to protect the organism, and therefore always register change of state not just descriptively, but also as an assessment of benefit or harm to bodily function and integrity. The consciousness that arises from this self-monitoring thus essentially involves this evaluative dimension, which is experienced in terms of feelings and emotions. By contrast, he says, our representations of external objects do not in themselves have an affective valence of this sort; this is something that is added by our representation of their effect on the organism.

Both the immunological and neurological views tie the concept of self to embodiment in an environment through its origins in mechanisms for the preservation of the organism in the face of environmental challenges. A different kind of argument for thinking of selves as fundamentally embodied beings is found in the phenomenological tradition. Phenomenologists do not start from scientific investigations into the biological origins of the self, but instead from our everyday experience of self and world. The phenomenological method is to reflect on the structure of ordinary experience and ask what the world and our relation to it must be for this experience to be as it is. One thing we discover by following this method, phenomenologists say, is that we always experience ourselves in a world of objects that can be seen, felt, and manipulated. We are not pure experiencing subjects that happen to encounter a world; we are necessarily experiencers *of* a world of objects. The phenomenological approach insists that experiencing objects as objects is not just a passive reception of sensory input from the outside. It is instead an active encounter with a world that we move through and interact with. An object is something that can be investigated and experienced from multiple perspectives. I can come closer to an object or move farther away. I can walk around it to see the other side, touch it to see how it feels, and so on. Our experience of objects as objects comes from the fact that we can and do experience them in multiple ways. We thus encounter objects as things which transcend particular experiences of them. What is given directly to the senses is only part of the object since it presents only one of the perspectives from which the object can be encountered. Yet we experience it *as* an entire object.

Crucially, our interaction with objects does not amount simply to sensing them from different points of view. More fundamentally, it is engaging them as entities with practical significance. In everyday life we do not first experience the objects around us as lumps of matter with particular characteristics, but as things with a purpose. I don't see a smooth brass-colored object, but a doorknob that can be grasped; not a cylindrical white object, but a mug from which I can drink; not a rectangular piece of plastic, but a credit card I can use to make purchases. Not every object is an artifact with a designed purpose, of course, but this general principle also holds true, perhaps in an even more basic sense, with natural objects. The tree can provide shade; the mushroom can be eaten; the boulder is in our way so we will need to change direction; the lightning is dangerous.

On this account, the self is given in experience as its subject. You will recall that in Chapter 4 we learned that phenomenologists see subject-less experience as incoherent. They thus hold that the experience of self arises in connection with the simultaneous experience of the world of which it is aware. The self is given as the invariant constant in our multiplicitous experience of the world. If an object can be encountered as a single thing that produces different experiences when I am close or far, when I walk around it, or pick it up, or tap it to hear what sound it makes, there must be a single subject that takes in all these different perspectives. Without this there could be no awareness of objects as entities that transcend individual experiences of them. The experience of an external world is thus simultaneously the experience of oneself as subject. Subject and object arise together as part of an experiential whole, and neither is possible without the other. Embodiment is part of the equation because our means of interacting with the world, and so of experiencing world and self, are sensory and embodied. The very ideas of a subjective "perspective" or "first-person point of view," so often evoked in discussions of the self, are metaphors for our experience of the world as encountered from a particular vantage point, evoking a physical location from which things appear as, for instance, reachable rather than unreachable.

The phenomenological argument for the embodied nature of selves has a different starting point from the immunological and neurological approaches, but all three share a common departure from a traditional starting point in which the self is understood as something sharply distinguished from the body. These views do not imply that selves simply *are* bodies. The point is rather that our concept of self and the experience that is taken to define it have their origins in facts about our embodiment and our interactions with an external environment, and so selves must be understood as embodied beings embedded in a world.

Social selves

If the self exists only through engagement with a world, an especially important part of that world is other selves, and the social dimensions of selfhood deserve special attention. The idea that social interactions are critical to selfhood and that selves are by their nature embedded in and formed by a social world has come up several times already. Indeed, social factors are connected to selves in so many ways and at so many different levels that it would be difficult to list them all. Here it is possible only to offer a brief description of some of the reasons that have been given for thinking that the self can only be understood within the context of a social world in which it interacts with others.

One widely discussed aspect of the role of the connection between selves and a social world is the way in which the attitudes and actions of others affect the development and formation of a true or authentic self. We saw examples of this in Chapter 3, where we considered ways in which oppressive social forces might interfere with the possibility of being one's true self while supportive social forces might enable authenticity. Jane's ability to realize herself as a mathematician was, we suggested, potentially dependent on the support of friends and mentors and complicated or stymied by the disapproval of her family. To see the authentic self as *essentially* social, however, is to say something more than simply that others can help us or hinder us in *expressing* who we truly are. The idea is that acceptance or recognition by others is part of what *makes* a particular feature part of who one truly is. When such recognition is not available, on this view, certain identities are not only difficult to express, but impossible to have.

The sense of "impossibility" behind this claim needs some unpacking. One way in which social norms and attitudes determine who someone can be is by placing constraints on what counts as a coherent identity. To see how this might work think, for instance, of the discussion of the narrative development of the self in Chapter 4. If we become selves by being taught to experience our lives as stories, this teaching at the same time provides a repertoire of particular kinds of stories that people (or people "like us") live, delimiting the kinds of selves we can be. This is not to say, of course, that social norms are completely determinative of who someone is nor that they can never be resisted or changed. We have countless historical examples of such change and resistance. What it does suggest, however, is that bringing about such change requires engaging and altering the relevant social world. Philosopher Hilde Lindemann, who defends a narrative account of identity, offers a detailed account of the ways in which social "master narratives" can make certain identities impossible, and how "counternarratives" can alter the space of possibilities, provided they get sufficient uptake. The impossible can become possible on this view, but only by changing the social environment.

The claim that social recognition is necessary for the development of a true self, when understood in this way, does not assume that social acceptance has magical powers that confer an identity without changing anything else. It is connected instead to an idea we have seen before; that who one is depends not only on some internal set of traits and thoughts that one may or may not express, but also on lived activities and interactions with others.

This idea was at work in Chapter 2, where we saw that everyday cases of "becoming someone else" towards the literal end of the spectrum are those in which the thread of a lived life, especially interpersonal relationships, is disrupted. It is present also in the objections to the "chosen self" view we discussed in Chapter 3. This is not to deny that people may have beliefs, values, and desires that are in some way natural and important to them and which, either through choice or lack of opportunity, they might fail to express. Nor does it imply that any social disapproval at all automatically undermines an authentic identity. The claim is rather that the development of our talents, desires, and values into an authentic self is something that happens over time and depends on what we do as well as on what we think and feel. To the extent that social context encourages, complicates, mandates, or blocks certain ways of life and forms of interaction, it therefore affects the selves we can and do develop into.

There is an extreme version of this idea, which does deny that there is anything to the self beyond social interactions. This is found in "performative" views of the self. Such an account is famously defended, for instance, by sociologist Erving Goffman. According to Goffman, human behavior is best understood in theatrical terms, as a series of performances. When we present ourselves in public, we act out roles appropriate to the audience and context in which we find ourselves in a manner that aims at eliciting a positive evaluation. The clothes we wear, our physical posture, and style of speech will vary with social context. In the classroom one might enact the role of professor; in the restaurant of customer; on the airplane of traveler, and so on. According to Goffman, this makes someone, in an important sense, a different self in each of these contexts. That people behave differently in different social situations is not a particularly ground-shaking revelation. The radical feature of Goffman's view is his insistence that these different "masks" or "performances" do not occlude a true self that is hidden behind them; they are all there is. The self is nothing more than the series of performances. This fact does not imply that we are necessarily alienated from what we are doing, or insincere in our self-presentations, or even that we self-consciously undertake to play a part. Performing the role of "clubgoer," for instance, requires nothing more than dressing up, going to the club, ordering a drink, and dancing. This might be something we really want to do, and which feels totally spontaneous, but it is an activity that is necessarily infused with social norms we are aiming to meet, and of which we are not the original authors.

Judith Butler offers another well-known performative view of self, focusing especially on gender as performance. Butler, too, emphasizes that there is no "truth" about the self that might be either expressed or misrepresented in our actions. The self, on her view, consists in the performance of social roles. There is no self without such performances, and hence no true self that could be liberated by removing it entirely from social norms and expectations so that it could just "be what it is." She therefore argues that what is necessary to support individual well-being is to allow for a broader range of roles to be enacted and to be more tolerant and supportive of different styles of enacting them. Rather than asking whether someone is "really" a man or a woman, gay, or straight, or queer, we should accept all of these as roles that an individual can choose to perform and recognize the self they represent as who they are. Performative views are by no means uncontroversial, but they do put into sharp relief a thought found also in less extreme accounts of the social nature of the self, that patterns of social interaction are not contingent features of the true self but part of what constitutes it. Recognizing this connection emphasizes the depth of the damage that can be done by social organizations that are discriminatory or systematically biased and underscores the ethical urgency of recognizing and addressing such social structures.

Another line of thought about the social nature of selves focuses less on the role of social influences in allowing the authenticity of self and more on ways in which selves depend upon a social context for their very existence. One relatively straightforward form of dependence was described in our discussion of human psychological development in Chapter 4. There we saw the critical role of caretakers, peers, and a broader social world in bringing a mature self into being and maintaining it once it has emerged. The intervention of caregivers is required for the development of the biological and cognitive features associated with selfhood. Infants who are not talked to, touched, and played with do not develop physically, cognitively, or emotionally in the same way as those who are. Beyond infancy, we saw evidence that children require social scaffolding to reach developmental milestones and gain the characteristics of mature human selves. Here the question is not about developing authentically or being who one truly is deep down, but rather about having the basic cognitive and agential capacities that make someone a human self in a more basic, fundamental sense. To the extent that the development of these capacities depends upon others, a social world is necessary for mature human selves to exist.

It might seem that this is not a terrifically deep point about selves in general, but only a contingent fact about how human selves develop. It so happens that *we* require social interactions, but this does not imply that all selves, even selves very like us, must. Perhaps technological advancements will one day allow the development of the self to take place through direct mechanical stimulation of the brain. Or maybe bio-cyborgs will be developed that are created as mature selves, or space exploration will yield encounters with alien races whose young, unlike human infants, are born with the full complement of cognitive and emotional capacities of typical adult humans. If we look more closely, however, the story of the development of the mature self in Chapter 4 points to a less contingent connection between selves and the social world. This connection is present not only in the mechanisms that allow humans to reach the relevant milestones en route to full-blown selfhood, but in the milestones themselves.

To develop into a mature self, as we saw, a child must come to recognize that the self she experiences internally is also an object for other selves (this is what the sticker test is supposed to show) and that other humans are distinct and independent subjects of experience (this is what the ability to attribute false beliefs is taken to show). The further developmental task of adolescence and beyond is to distinguish one's own traits, proclivities, values, and goals from those of one's family, community, and friends and to carve out a unique narrative path.

All these milestones presuppose the existence of others from whom one gradually comes to distinguish oneself in increasingly subtle and sophisticated ways. Recall Locke's "forensic" definition of selves as beings with the capacity for reflective self-consciousness, who are legitimate objects of praise, blame, punishment, and reward. According to a central understanding of human development, the kind of reflective self-consciousness Locke describes is accomplished precisely by coming to recognize oneself as an individual subject whose own inner life is distinct from that of others. Fittingness as an object of praise or blame, at the very least, presupposes interactions with others (or at least one other) that are governed by rules and moral laws. All of this suggests that part of what it *means* to become a mature self is to take one's place as a unique individual in a social world. Even if our imagined aliens were born with all the cognitive capacities of an adult human self and had no need for the help of others to obtain them, their continued existence as selves would require a social context.

It is telling that periods of profound and prolonged isolation tend to cause disturbances of the self not unlike some of those described in Chapter 5. Without others with whom one interacts and in contrast to whom one defines oneself, it is difficult to retain an integrated sense of self-awareness. Prolonged social deprivation has profound effects on subjectivity, as many people learned during the lockdowns of the Covid-19 pandemic. When people are cut off from human contact for long periods of time, they tend to create imagined others to simulate a social world in something like the way protagonist Chuck Noland (Tom Hanks) does in the Hollywood film *Cast Away*. Stranded on a deserted island after a plane crash, Noland paints a face on a volleyball and names it Wilson. Throughout his isolation he speaks to Wilson as if to another person, and this imaginative exercise helps him retain his sanity and hold himself together.

A different but related position argues that individual selves can only be understood as abstractions from a community or social world. This claim is often connected with an argument that the idea of an independent, atomistic self is an artifact of a particular sociohistorical context. If we take a broader perspective, proponents of this view say, we will find cultures and eras in which the "we" is seen as more fundamental than the "I." This idea is expressed, for instance, in the African concept of "ubuntu," which is often translated as "I am because we are." Archbishop Desmond Tutu, who helped popularize this philosophy in parts of the world in which it had been less well known, glosses it as the view that we "belong in a bundle of life," and that "a person is a person through other persons." This general perspective is expressed also in many feminist views that argue for a more relational conception of self and agency than those they see as standard in modern, industrialized societies.

Exactly what it means to say that the "we" comes before the "I" is a complicated question, and this idea is unpacked in different ways by different thinkers in different contexts. One interpretation sees the priority of the "we" in fundamentally moral terms. Understood this way, the claim that the "we" comes before the "I" amounts to the ethical position that the good of the community is (or should be) more important than the good of the individuals who make it up. Cultures in which the "we" comes first in this sense are ones in which individuals regularly put the needs and aims of the community before their own. This reading does not necessarily imply that individual selves depend on community for their existence, only that the value of community is greater.

Claims about the priority of the "we" might also, however, be taken to imply something stronger. On the stronger interpretation it is not just that it is one's personal duty to put the well-being of the collective above one's own personal well-being. The thought is rather that there is a real and important sense in which the well-being of the community is more fundamentally *one's own* well-being than is that of the individual self, that one is more fundamentally a part of the community than an individual. To make sense of this we can think about how an analogous claim would work within a single human life. A "teenaged self" is a perfectly useful unit. We can talk about someone's "teenaged self" and how it differs from his "childhood self" or "adult self." The teenaged self may, moreover, have its own interests and goals, quite distinct from those of other portions of his life (e.g., the "middle-aged self"), and perhaps in tension with them. Many would argue, however, that it is shortsighted for a teenager to pursue his current interests without regard to those of his middle-aged self. If he acts to fulfill his teenaged goals and desires in ways that undermine adult possibilities, according to this common view, he is being imprudent, not immoral. Actions that allow his adult self to flourish are not altruistic; in taking them he has done something good for himself. This judgment rests on the assumption that the teenaged self is not a truly independent being, but one part of a more basic unit, an entire human life. It can be useful for some purposes to talk about "teenaged" or "middle-aged" selves as if they were independent units, but in fact they are abstractions and not genuinely independent entities.

Claims about the priority of the "we" can be read as saying that the whole of an individual human life is still not a broad enough perspective from which to consider what ultimately constitutes one's own well-being, and so one's actual limits. The individual human self, according to this view, is a part of the community in much the same way that the teenaged self is part of the human self, and for similar reasons. We see the teenaged self as a part of a larger life because there could be no teenaged self without the life in which it inheres. The teenager's story started before he turned 13 and will continue after he turns 20. Who he is now flows from his childhood and will flow into and influence his adulthood. In much the same way, those who urge the priority of the "we" might argue, the story of an individual human self flows from what came before their birth and will flow into and influence what comes after. In addition, individual human stories are inextricably tied up with those of others in the present, and so of the broader social world they inhabit. In this sense the community can be seen as metaphysically prior to individual human selves.

Different instances of this view vary with respect to how broadly they conceive the community of which the individual self is an abstract part. Some versions see it as a local or targeted group. The picture might be, for instance, that your story began with your Capulet ancestors and will continue in your descendants. The glories of earlier Capulets redound to you, as insults to earlier Capulets are insults to *you*, which must be avenged when you encounter the descendants of the Montague who insulted the earlier Capulet, even at the expense of your own individual life. In this sense you are first and foremost a Capulet, and only secondarily the individual Capulet that you are. A similar story might be told about one's relations to other kinds of communities, for example, tribe, country, religious group, laborers for a common cause. Some see the relevant "we" as the entire human race. This sentiment is expressed, for instance, in John Donne's famous lines: "no man is an island entire of itself; every man is a piece of the continent; a part of the main."

This brief survey of different ways in which the self might be seen to require, or even be constituted by, a social world has barely scratched the surface of the complex ways in which the self might be considered a necessarily social being. The multiple forms of connection between self and society continue to be hotly debated, and a great deal of controversy remains. Nevertheless, there seem clear reasons for at least acknowledging a direct and intimate connection between the very concept of a self and a social world, even as we continue to debate the details of this connection.

In this chapter, we have looked at different ways in which the nature of individual selves and the existence of selves as a kind might be dependent upon engagement with a social and natural world. This discussion paints a picture of the self in which the social and natural environment is more like the medium in which selves exist than a set of circumstances in which they might or might not find themselves. Selves, from this perspective, are not inert objects defined by a set of essential attributes. They are dynamic subjects and agents, living a life filled with experiences, choices, emotions, activities, and relationships. This suggests that to fully understand and describe their nature we will need to recognize and attend to these dynamics and to the kind of environment required for them to occur.

Where we have ended up might seem very far from the conception of the self as a unified subject of experiences with which we began in Chapter 1. But the distance may be less, or at least of a different sort, than it first appears. Over the course of our discussion one thing has become clear: the nature of the self is immensely complex. This is not surprising given the centrality of selves in our existence. We *are* selves, after all, and interaction with other selves is, if nothing else, a large part of most people's daily lives. Talk of different "kinds" of self (e.g., the true self, the minimal self, the metaphysical self), or questions about the nature of the self (e.g., what kind of unity does it require? Under what circumstances does the same self continue?) might thus be understood not as addressing distinct topics, but rather as emphasizing and exploring different aspects of a single topic and thereby revealing different perspectives on and interests in a single phenomenon.

We have discovered time and again that the different characterizations of the self, as well as the various questions about its integrity and persistence, are ultimately entangled. It can be useful at the start to distinguish these characterizations and to address the different questions independently. When we do, however, investigation of one seems to lead inexorably to the others. We thus need not take the conclusion that embodiment and a social and natural environment are critical to the self's existence or continuity as implying that the view of the self as a unified and discrete subject of experience is simply false. Instead, we can take it as an invitation to think more deeply about the nature of the unity and experience we take to constitute the self, what might be required to allow for it, and what other features of self are entailed by it. Nothing we have seen forces us to give up the idea that a self is a unified, experiencing subject. It might, however, lead us to conclude the self is not *just* that and that unified experiencing subjects are more complexly structured than we initially thought.

Following different threads of investigation into the self has helped us appreciate the many ways in which these threads are interwoven, allowing a subtle, textured, and somewhat untidy picture of who and what we are to emerge. Recognizing this explains why the oracle's injunction to know ourselves is so difficult, but also why undertaking it is so fascinating and rewarding.

References and further reading

Chapter 1: The metaphysical self

References

Chalmers, D. J. (1995). "Facing Up to the Problem of Consciousness." *Journal of Consciousness Studies* 2: 200–19.

Hume, D. (1978). *Treatise of Human Nature*, ed. L. A. Selby-Bigge (2nd edn.). Oxford: Oxford University Press.

Locke, J. (1975). *Essay Concerning Human Understanding*, ed. P. H. Nidditch. Oxford: Oxford University Press.

Parfit, D. A. (1984). *Reasons and Persons*. Oxford: Oxford University Press.

Further reading

Dennett, D. (2017). "Where am I?" In *Brainstorms*. Cambridge, MA: MIT Press, pp. 333–46.

Descartes, R. (2008). *Meditations on First Philosophy*, trans. M. Moriarty. Oxford: Oxford University Press.

James, W. (1918). *The Principles of Psychology*. New York: H. Holt.

Keown, D. (2013). *Buddhism: A Very Short Introduction*. Oxford: Oxford University Press.

Metzinger, T. (2009). *The Ego Tunnel: The Science of the Mind and the Myth of the Self*. New York: Basic Books.

Montero, B. (2022). *Philosophy of Mind: A Very Short Introduction*. Oxford: Oxford University Press.

Mumford, S. (2012). "What is a Person?" In *Metaphysics: A Very Short Introduction*. Oxford: Oxford University Press, pp. 65–75.

Perry, John (1977). *A Dialogue on Personal Identity and Immortality*. London: Hackett.

Strawson, G. (2004). "Against Narrativity." *Ratio* 17/4: 428–52.

Wilkes, K. V. (1988). *Real People: Personal Identity without Thought Experiments*. Oxford: Oxford University Press.

Chapter 2: Becoming someone else

References

"Deep Impact; Treating Depression." *Economist* 374/8416 (March 5, 2005).

Gilbert, F., et al. (2017). "I Miss Being Me: Phenomenological Effects of Deep Brain Stimulation." *AJOB Neuroscience* 8/2: 96–109. DOI: 10.1080/21507740.2017.1320319.

Ibsen, H., and Rudall, N. (1999). *A Doll's House*. Chicago: I. R. Dee.

O'Connor, J. "A Different Person Came Back." *National Post* online, <http://afghanistan.nationalpost.com/%E2%80%98a-different-person-came-back%E2%80%99/>, posted July 9, 2011, accessed Mar. 16, 2013.

Parfit, D. A. (1984). *Reasons and Persons*. Oxford: Oxford University Press.

Schechtman, M. (2010). "Philosophical Reflections on Narrative and Deep Brain Stimulation." *The Journal of Clinical Ethics* 21/2: 133–9.

Further reading

Brison, S. J. (2011). *Aftermath: Violence and the Remaking of a Self*. Princeton: Princeton University Press, pp. 1–165.

Kramer, P. D. (1994). *Listening to Prozac*. New York: Penguin Books.

Chapter 3: Being who you are

References

Freud, S. (2014). *Civilization and its Discontents*. London: Penguin Classics.

Hobbes, T. (2008). *Leviathan*, ed. J. C. A. Gaskin. Oxford: Oxford University Press.

Nietzsche, F. (1998). *On the Genealogy of Morality*, trans. M. Clark and A. J. Swensen. London: Hackett.

Rowling, J. K. (1998). *Harry Potter and the Chamber of Secrets*. New York: Scholastic Press, p. 333.

Further reading

Frankfurt, H. (1988). *The Importance of What We Care About*. Cambridge: Cambridge University Press.

Korsgaard, C. M. (1996). *The Sources of Normativity*. Cambridge: Cambridge University Press.

Mackenzie, C. (2021). "Relational Autonomy." In K. Q. Hall and Ásta (eds.), *The Oxford Handbook of Feminist Philosophy*. New York: Oxford University Press, pp. 374–84.

McAdams, D. P. (1993). *The Stories We Live by: Personal Myths and the Making of the Self*. Houston, TX: William Morrow & Co.

Newman, G., De Freitas, J., and Knobe, J. (2015). "Beliefs about the True Self Explain Asymmetries Based on Moral Judgment." *Cognitive Science* 39: 96–125.

Schechtman, M. (2011). "The Narrative Self." In Shaun Gallagher (ed.), *The Oxford Handbook of the Self*. Oxford: Oxford University Press.

Chapter 4: Waxing and waning selves

References

James, W. (1918). *The Principles of Psychology*. New York: H. Holt.

Zahavi, D. (2010). "Minimal Self and Narrative Self: A Distinction in Need of Refinement." In Thomas Fuchs, Heribert Sattel, and Peter Henningsen (eds.), *The Embodied Self: Dimensions, Coherence, and Disorders*. Stuttgart: Schattauer, pp. 3–11.

Further reading

Animal Cognition. *Lists of Animals That Have Passed the Mirror Test*. <https://www.animalcognition.org/2015/04/15/list-of-animals-that-have-passed-the-mirror-test/>. Accessed Oct. 20, 2022.

Coulmas, C. (2019). "Selfhood and Personality: The Psychology of Identity." In *Identity: A Very Short Introduction*. Oxford: Oxford University Press, pp. 89–100.

McAdams, D. P. (1994). *The Person: An Introduction to Personality Psychology* (2nd edn.). Fort Worth, TX: Harcourt Brace.

McLean, K. C. (2016). *The Co-authored Self: Family Stories and the Construction of Personal Identity*. Oxford: Oxford University Press.

Mischel, W. (2014). *The Marshmallow Test: Mastering Self-control*. Boston: Little, Brown, and Co.

Nelson, K., and Fivush, R. (2020). "The Development of Autobiographical Memory, Autobiographical Narratives, and Autobiographical Consciousness." *Psychological Reports* 123/1: 71–96. <https://doi.org/10.1177/0033294119852574>.

Chapter 5: Divided and distressed selves

References

American Psychiatric Association (2013). *Diagnostic and Statistical Manual of Mental Disorders* (5th edn.). <https://doi.org/10.1176/appi.books.9780890425596>.

Dissociative Identity Disorder Research Organization. "Cooperation, Integration, and Fusion." <https://did-research.org/treatment/integration>. Accessed July 7, 2023.

Locke, J. (1975). *Essay Concerning Human Understanding*, ed. P. H. Nidditch. Oxford: Oxford University Press.

Nagel, T. (1971). "Brain Bisection and the Unity of Consciousness." *Synthese* 22/3–4: 396–413. <http://www.jstor.org/stable/20114764>.

Ratcliffe, M., and Wilkinson, S. (2015). "Thought Insertion Clarified." *Journal of Consciousness Studies* 22/11–12: 246–69.

Sacks, O. (1985). "The Man Who Fell Out of Bed." In *The Man Who Mistook His Wife for a Hat and Other Clinical Tales*. New York: Summit Books, pp. 66–70.

Sierra, M., and David, A. S. (2011). "Depersonalization: A Selective Impairment of Self-awareness." *Consciousness and Cognition* 20/1: 99–108. <https://doi.org/10.1016/j.concog.2010.10.018>.

Further reading

de Haan, E. H. F., Corballis, P. M., Hillyard, S. A., et al. (2020). "Split-Brain: What We Know Now and Why This is Important for Understanding Consciousness." *Neuropsychol. Rev.* 30: 224–33. <https://doi.org/10.1007/s11065-020-09439-3>.

Dorahy, M. J., Brand, B. L., Sar, V., Krüger, C., Stavropoulos, P., Martínez-Taboas, A., Lewis-Fernández, R., and Middleton, W. (2014). "Dissociative Identity Disorder: An Empirical Overview." *Aust. NZ J. Psychiatry* 48/5: 402–17. DOI: 10.1177/0004867414527523. PMID: 24788904.

Gallagher, S. (2015). "Relations between Agency and Ownership in the Case of Schizophrenic Thought Insertion and Delusions of Control." *Review of Philosophy and Psychology* 6/4: 865–79.

Grazino, M. (2016). "The Brain Damage That Hides Half the World." *The Atlantic*.

Parton, A., Malhotra, P., and Husain, M. (2004). "Hemispatial Neglect." *Journal of Neurology, Neurosurgery & Psychiatry* 75: 13–21.

Theravive, "Dissociative Identity Disorder (DID) DSM-5 300.14 (F44.81)." <https://www.theravive.com/therapedia/dissociative-identity-disorder-(did)-dsm-5–300.14-(f44.81).> Accessed July 9, 2023.

Chapter 6: Embodied, social selves

References

Butler, J. (1990). "Performative Acts and Gender Constitution: An Essay in Phenomenology and Feminist Theory." In Sue-Ellen Case (ed.), *Performing Feminisms: Feminist Critical Theory and Theatre.* Baltimore: Johns Hopkins University Press.

Damasio, A. R. (1994). *Descartes' Error: Emotion, Reason, and the Human Brain.* New York: G. P. Putnam.

Damasio, A. R. (2014) "What is the Self?" YouTube video, <https://www.youtube.com/watch?v=Jkl1qnnx5mo>. Accessed Oct. 19, 2022.

Donne, J. "No Man Is an Island." *All Poetry,* <https://allpoetry.com/No-man-is-an-island>. Accessed Oct. 20, 2022.

Goffman, E. (1959). *The Presentation of Self in Everyday Life.* New York: Bantam Doubleday Dell Publishing Group.

Lindemann, Hilde (2014). *Holding and Letting Go: The Social Practice of Personal Identities.* New York: OUP USA.

Tutu, D. (2011). "'Ubuntu': On the Nature of Human Community." In *God Is Not a Christian: And Other Provocations.* New York: HarperOne, pp. 21–4.

Further reading

Coulmas, F. (2019). *Identity: A Very Short Introduction.* Oxford: Oxford University Press.

Gallagher, S. (2012). *Phenomenology.* New York: Palgrave Macmillan.

Rattansi, A. (2020). *Racism: A Very Short Introduction.* Oxford: Oxford University Press.

Sánchez-Ramón, S., and Faure, F. (2020). "Self and the Brain: The Immune Metaphor." *Frontiers in Psychiatry* 11: 540, 676. <https://doi.org/10.3389/fpsyt.2020.540676>.

Zahavi, D. (2018). *Phenomenology: The Basics.* Oxford: Routledge.

Index

For the benefit of digital users, indexed terms that span two pages (e.g., 52–53) may, on occasion, appear on only one of those pages.

The Self

ADVERTISING
A Very Short Introduction
Winston Fletcher

The book contains a short history of advertising and an explanation of how the industry works, and how each of the parties (the advertisers , the media and the agencies) are involved. It considers the extensive spectrum of advertisers and their individual needs. It also looks at the financial side of advertising and asks how advertisers know if they have been successful, or whether the money they have spent has in fact been wasted. Fletcher concludes with a discussion about the controversial and unacceptable areas of advertising such as advertising products to children and advertising products such as cigarettes and alcohol. He also discusses the benefits of advertising and what the future may hold for the industry.

www.oup.com/vsi

AGEING
A Very Short Introduction
Nancy A. Pachana

Ageing is an activity we are familiar with from an early age.
In our younger years upcoming birthdays are anticipated with
an excitement that somewhat diminishes as the years progress.
As we grow older we are bombarded with advice on ways to
overcome, thwart, resist, and, on the rare occasion, embrace,
one's ageing. Have all human beings from the various historical
epochs and cultures viewed ageing with this same ambivalence?

In this *Very Short Introduction* Nancy A. Pachana discusses the
lifelong dynamic changes in biological, psychological, and social
functioning involved in ageing. Increased lifespans in the
developed and the developing world have created an urgent need
to find ways to enhance our well-being in the later decades of life.
This need is reflected in policies and action plans addressing our
ageing populations from the World Health Organization and the
United Nations.

BEHAVIOURAL ECONOMICS
A Very Short Introduction
Michelle Baddeley

Traditionally economists have based their economic predictions on the assumption that humans are super-rational creatures, using the information we are given efficiently and generally making selfish decisions that work well for us as individuals. Economists also assume that we're doing the very best we can possibly do—not only for today, but over our whole lifetimes too. Increasingly, however, the study of behavioural economics is revealing that our lives are not that simple. Instead, our decisions are complicated by our own psychology. Each of us makes mistakes every day. We don't always know what's best for us and, even if we do, we might not have the self-control to deliver on our best intentions. We struggle to stay on diets, to get enough exercise, and to manage our money.

This *Very Short Introduction* explores the reasons why we make irrational decisions; how we decide quickly; why we make mistakes in risky situations; our tendency to procrastinate; and how we are affected by social influences, personality, mood, and emotions. As Michelle Baddeley explains, the implications of understanding the rationale for our own financial behaviour are huge. She concludes by looking forward, to see what the future of behavioural economics holds for us.

www.oup.com/vsi

COGNITIVE NEUROSCIENCE
A Very Short Introduction
Richard Passingham

Up to the 1960s, psychology regarded what happened within the mind as scientifically unapproachable. As medical research evolved, outlines of brain components and processes began to take shape, and by the end of the 1970s, a new science, cognitive neuroscience, was born.

In this *Very Short Introduction*, distinguished cognitive neuroscientist Richard Passingham gives a provocative and exciting account of the nature and scope of this relatively new field. He explains what brain imaging shows, pointing out common misconceptions, and gives a brief overview of the different aspects of human cognition: perceiving, attending, remembering, reasoning, deciding, and acting. He also considers the exciting advances that may lie ahead.

CONSCIENCE
A Very Short Introduction
Paul Strohm

In the West conscience has been relied upon for two thousand years as a judgement that distinguishes right from wrong. It has effortlessly moved through every period division and timeline between the ancient, medieval, and modern. The Romans identified it, the early Christians appropriated it, and Reformation Protestants and loyal Catholics relied upon its advice and admonition. Today it is embraced with equal conviction by non-religious and religious alike. Considering its deep historical roots and exploring what it has meant to successive generations, Paul Strohm highlights why this particularly European concept deserves its reputation as 'one of the prouder Western contributions to human rights and human dignity throughout the world.

www.oup.com/vsi

ENGLISH LITERATURE

A Very Short Introduction

Jonathan Bate

Sweeping across two millennia and every literary genre, acclaimed scholar and biographer Jonathan Bate provides a dazzling introduction to English Literature. The focus is wide, shifting from the birth of the novel and the brilliance of English comedy to the deep Englishness of landscape poetry and the ethnic diversity of Britain's Nobel literature laureates. It goes on to provide a more in-depth analysis, with close readings from an extraordinary scene in King Lear to a war poem by Carol Ann Duffy, and a series of striking examples of how literary texts change as they are transmitted from writer to reader.

{No reviews}

www.oup.com/vsi

FILM
A Very Short Introduction
Michael Wood

Film is considered by some to be the most dominant art form of the twentieth century. It is many things, but it has become above all a means of telling stories through images and sounds. The stories are often offered to us as quite false, frankly and beautifully fantastic, and they are sometimes insistently said to be true. But they are stories in both cases, and there are very few films, even in avant-garde art, that don't imply or quietly slip into narrative. This story element is important, and is closely connected with the simplest fact about moving pictures: they do move. In this *Very Short Introduction* Michael Wood provides a brief history and examination of the nature of the medium of film, considering its role and impact on society as well as its future in the digital age.

GLOBALIZATION
A Very Short Introduction
Manfred Steger

'Globalization' has become one of the defining buzzwords of our time - a term that describes a variety of accelerating economic, political, cultural, ideological, and environmental processes that are rapidly altering our experience of the world. It is by its nature a dynamic topic - and this *Very Short Introduction* has been fully updated for 2009, to include developments in global politics, the impact of terrorism, and environmental issues. Presenting globalization in accessible language as a multifaceted process encompassing global, regional, and local aspects of social life, Manfred B. Steger looks at its causes and effects, examines whether it is a new phenomenon, and explores the question of whether, ultimately, globalization is a good or a bad thing.

www.oup.com/vsi

JUNG
A Very Short Introduction
Anthony Stevens

Anthony Stevens argues that Jung's visionary powers and profound spirituality have helped many to find an alternative set of values to the arid materialism prevailing in Western society.

This concise introduction explains clearly the basic concepts of Jungian philosophy: the collective unconscious, complex, archetype, shadow, persona, anima, animus, and the individuation of the Self. Anthony Stevens examines Jung's views on such disparate subjects as myth, religion, alchemy, 'synchronicity', and the psychology of gender differences. He devotes separate chapters to the stages of life, Jung's theory of psychological types, the interpretation of dreams, the practice of Jungian analysis, and to the unjust allegation that Jung was a Nazi sympathizer.

'Jung's relations with Freud and the contrasts between their psychologies form a fascinating backdrop to this accessible, authoritative but, above all, very readable little book.'

Clinical Psychology Forum

'Offers a concise introduction to Jungian psychology, covering everything from the collective unconscious and the archetype to the theories of synchronicity and individuation.'

Calgary Herald

www.oup.com/vsi

MEMORY
A Very Short Introduction
Michael J. Benton

Why do we remember events from our childhood as if they
happened yesterday, but not what we did last week? Why does
our memory seem to work well sometimes and not others?
What happens when it goes wrong? Can memory be improved
or manipulated, by psychological techniques or even 'brain
implants'? How does memory grow and change as we age?
And what of so-called 'recovered' memories? This book brings
together the latest research in neuroscience and psychology,
and weaves in case-studies, anecdotes, and even literature
and philosophy, to address these and many other important
questions about the science of memory - how it works,
and why we can't live without it.

www.oup.com/vsi

THE BODY
A Very Short Introduction
Chris Shilling

The human body is thought of conventionally as a biological entity, with its longevity, morbidity, size and even appearance determined by genetic factors immune to the influence of society or culture. Since the mid-1980s, however, there has been a rising awareness of how our bodies, and our perception of them, are influenced by the social, cultural and material contexts in which humans live.

Drawing on studies of sex and gender, education, governance, the economy, and religion, Chris Shilling demonstrates how our physical being allows us to affect the material and virtual world around us, yet also enables governments to shape and direct our thoughts and actions. Revealing how social relationships, cultural images, and technological and medical advances shape our perceptions and awareness, he exposes the limitations of traditional Western traditions of thought that elevate the mind over the body as that which defines us as human. Dealing with issues ranging from cosmetic and transplant surgery, the performance of gendered identities, the commodification of bodies and body parts, and the violent consequences of competing conceptions of the body as sacred, Shilling provides a compelling account of why body matters present contemporary societies with a series of urgent and inescapable challenges.

THE MEANING OF LIFE
A Very Short Introduction
Terry Eagleton

'Philosophers have an infuriating habit of analysing questions rather than answering them', writes Terry Eagleton, who, in these pages, asks the most important question any of us ever ask, and attempts to answer it. So what is the meaning of life? In this witty, spirited, and stimulating inquiry, Eagleton shows how centuries of thinkers - from Shakespeare and Schopenhauer to Marx, Sartre and Beckett - have tackled the question. Refusing to settle for the bland and boring, Eagleton reveals with a mixture of humour and intellectual rigour how the question has become particularly problematic in modern times. Instead of addressing it head-on, we take refuge from the feelings of 'meaninglessness' in our lives by filling them with a multitude of different things: from football and sex, to New Age religions and fundamentalism.

'Light hearted but never flippant.'

The Guardian.

www.oup.com/vsi